For More Information Visit:
http://boyswontbeboys.com
614.496.1794

faydem.W

D1263840

Boys Won't Be Boys

Empowering Boys to Live Uncommon in a Common World

By Tim Brown

Copyright © 2013 by Tim Brown

Boys Won't Be Boys
Empowering Boys to Live Uncommon in a Common World
by Tim Brown

Printed in the United States of America

ISBN 9781628395785

All rights reserved solely by the author. The author guarantees all contents are original and do not infringe upon the legal rights of any other person or work. No part of this book may be reproduced in any form without the permission of the author. The views expressed in this book are not necessarily those of the publisher.

Unless otherwise indicated, Bible quotations are taken from The MESSAGE: The Bible in Contemporary Language. Copyright ©2002 by Eugene Peterson.

Unless otherwise indicated, Bible quotations are taken from the Holy Bible, New Living Translation. Copyright ©1996 by Tyndale House Publishers.

Unless otherwise indicated, Bible quotations are taken from The Holy Bible, English Standard Version. Copyright ©2001 by Crossway, a publishing ministry of Good News Publishers.

www.xulonpress.com

Edited by Shannah Hogue
Cover Design by Samuel Silverman

Acknowledgments

I want to thank my family for their support and encouragement throughout the writing of this book. My wife Karmen, and children, Timothy Jr., Karmell, and Nathaniel.

This book is dedicated to my mother Jewrett Bailey the woman with THE HAT.

Table of Contents

Foreword

Foreword to Boys Won't Be Boys by Tim Brown
Carey Casey

N ot long ago, I had the opportunity to interact with a group of six or seven teenage boys at a local detention center. They were all African-American, thirteen to fifteen years old. At the time it struck me that they were about the same age as my own son.

I know what they were thinking when I walked in. *Who's this joker?* And, *What does he want from me?*

I started asking them basic questions—their names, what did they do to get in trouble, that sort of thing. Most of them avoided my eyes when they talked.

Before long, being who I am, I had to ask about their dads. Fathers are always a huge factor. As you might expect, most of them didn't have involved dads.

One boy said defiantly, "I don't care about my dad. I don't want to see him. I don't even want to know about him."

I said, "That's interesting. So, do you want to have a son one day?"

He said, "Sure."

"Why?"

"So I can teach him stuff."

I looked around the room at the other boys. "Did you hear what he said? He wants to *be* something that he doesn't even *like* right now, something he doesn't want in his life." And then I said, "Guys, what's going on there?"

That idea seemed to break the ice. I tried—for just a few minutes— to be their dad and give them a better picture of what a dad can be. I desperately wanted them to know: *Fathers have value.* They had never considered that before! How could they even imagine or be aware of the rewards and joy of fatherhood? They've never seen it!

That interaction wasn't the most high-profile engagement I've ever had, but it was one of the most worthwhile. I affirmed those young men—verbally and physically, and I hope I helped them a bit. But I was reaffirmed too. I need those regular reminders of what happens when dads aren't around.

Everyone needs the influence of a father or father figure. I am very blessed to have a dad who was there for me. When I was growing up, Pop thought of himself as a philosopher. He liked to lay his profound thoughts on us kids, and then see us try to figure them out.

One of his favorite words was *watch.* He'd say, "Son, you must always *watch.*" And I'd be like, "C'mon, Pop, what do you mean, *Watch*? School me, Dad."

Eventually, I realized that *watch* was a warning, his way of saying, *Be careful. Don't take life lightly. Don't get hurt because you weren't paying attention to something important.*

Usually, we'd hear it when someone we knew got in trouble.

A young man in my hometown, one of the greatest athletes ever to come up, drowned in the river his senior year because he underestimated the currents. "*Watch,*" Pop told us.

A few years later, my cousin took off in his car late one night to meet some girls, even after his father told him it wasn't a good idea. He missed a turn, and it ended his life. "He wasn't *watching,*" my dad said.

Over and over, my dad would say, "Son, *watch.* Don't be in the wrong place at the wrong time and get your car shot at." "*Watch!* Don't be at some party where you don't need to be. *Watch!*"

Back then, I got tired of hearing it. But now, I see the value of him speaking truth into my life. He saved me from some difficult times and some big regrets.

The influence of a father is irreplaceable. We all need someone to teach us to *watch*. Young men, especially, need that kind of coaching as they move through life, mature and find their place in the world. In an ideal situation, every boy would have a great relationship with his dad, and the needed skills, attitudes, and values would be transferred from father to son as part of everyday life.

But sadly, that isn't happening for far too many young men. As was true for the boys in the detention center, many fathers are either physically absent or emotionally distant. Moms do their best to fill the gap, but boys need that guidance and accountability from their fathers.

That is why I am excited by the challenge issued in this book by my friend, Tim Brown. He is a man I greatly respect for being teachable, humble, and a real team player. And his book is a powerful tool that can help young boys who are struggling without the influence of a father.

Whether you have received life lessons from your father or a father figure— whether you're in your teens or a grown man like me— this book is a great source for clear insights about how to succeed in life: in work, friendships, faith, and relationships. You will benefit from the principles in this book. I urge you to come back to each chapter two or three times and really soak in the truths that you find. The advice in this book can help you shape a new future for yourself and for the boys who need the influence and challenge that Tim provides.

Endorsements

I've known Tim Brown for 40 years, and we've been friends for over 25 of those years. He's always had a servant's heart, particularly in mentoring young people, and especially young boys. His book covers important ground in seeking to help boys become "Uncommon Men". And he's covered that ground well.

Plain, Powerful, Practical talk for men of all ages. The call to action and challenge for boys and men to live uncommon lives is loud.. and the path, while not easy, has been clearly stated in the pages of this book. It is both a resource and roadmap for those ready to experience the adventure and rewards of being "Uncommon Men".

Clark Kellogg, CBS Sports Color Analyst

Tim Brown has written a challenging call to boys to help them transform their life from the common to Uncommon way of thinking and living. This book is the catalyst to begin the process to help turn the tide of future men to accept their responsibility as fathers and leaders. This book is a must read for boys and men who want to live an Uncommon Life and a Life of Significance.

Chris Spielman, NFL and OSU All-American, and ESPN College Football Analyst

Boys Won't Be Boys: Empowering Boys to Live Uncommon in a Common World is a clarion call to inspire young African American males to transcend the insidious mediocrity that has gripped this generation and is pervasive throughout our society. Tim Brown has condensed years of mentoring and ministry into a concise and straightforward volume that describes a blue print and roadmap to developing the tremendous potential these boys possess. It is a call to our young men to rise above the negative media portrayals of what a Black man is or should be and to live out the greatness that is within them. This book should be required reading for all young African American males and the adults who are charged with their development.

Robert L. Murphy-CEO/CAO, The Ted Ginn Sr. Masters Preparatory Academy

Tim Brown had taken his years of experience as a Father, Coach, Ministry leader, and most importantly scripture and woven it into a great inspirational and practical guide to developing young men. Every person who wants to make a difference in the lives of youth and/or wants to learn how to invest into the lives of others should read this book.

Al Schierbaum, State Director, Fellowship of Christian Athletes

"Instead of focusing on external statistical reasoning or third party research why young men are underperforming in life at an alarming rate, Boys Won't Be Boys purposely and successfully instructs young men how to recognize and neutralize negative internal thoughts, feelings and emotions that keep them living a "common" life.

Boys Won't Be Boys introduces and provides young men of all ages, backgrounds, ethnicities and cultures a safe, accountability training tool, to install into their hearts for use throughout their entire adult lives. If nothing else, after reading this book, young men will realize that going from common to uncommon starts with you (U)!"

Roy Hall, Former Ohio State and NFL Wide Receiver, and DRIVEN Foundation President

Chapter 1

Uncommon Foundation

Uncommon

There are just two paths through life.

Both paths are open to you. Both paths end up at the same place. And everyone in the world has to pick one of them...including you.

But there are only two options. And they are very, very different.

Taking the first path is like driving a four-lane highway in a sleek, red Dodge Charger. It is straight and smooth. You can put your car in drive and glide along on heated leather seats. Path #1 is an easy ride to your destination.

Path #2 is the opposite. It's a back country gravel road. With hills. And potholes. And you're driving it in a 1982 manual transmission pickup truck with no air conditioning. This road is anything but smooth. It's bumpy and dirty. And you have to think hard, work hard, and commit all the way to get to where you're going.

That's it. Two roads. Two ways to get through life. And you have to pick one.

So...which would you choose?

I'm willing to bet that your gut instinct is to take Path #1. Who wouldn't, right? Who doesn't want to drive a car like that all the way down Easy Street?

But that is exactly the problem. Almost everyone picks the first path. Path #1 is the Common path.

Path #1 is jam-packed. Sure, it's smooth, but you're stuck doing 35 mph in traffic as far as you can see. That hot ride should make you the center of attention, but everyone around you has the same car. You aren't special. You aren't a master of the road. You are just like everyone else.

But there is another option.

At first glance, Path #2 is rough and dirty. There's no swagger there. There's nothing flashy or smooth about it. But despite how it looks, Path #2 is the uncommon choice.

Most people do not choose the second path. Even though it takes more work to navigate, you can roll down the windows and barrel along, blasting music from the radio loud enough to scare the birds. You can fly, a cloud of dust behind you, free from the influence of everyone else. You are a master of the road. You are a master of your destiny. You are Uncommon.

These are your only two options: Common or Uncommon. Which one are you gonna be?

A Better Path

In real life, of course, we aren't talking about cars on the road. We're talking about you, how you live, the choices you make, and the way you deal with people.

Choosing the common life is the "safe" road. *Common* means looking like everyone else, acting like everyone else, and talking like everyone else. Common means blending in. It means you don't make waves. It means being a follower.

Being common is easy, too. And not in a good way. A common man doesn't work hard to succeed. Common means doing the bare minimum, taking the easy road, just squeaking by.

But most of all, common is shallow. It's all about image, about how you look on the outside. The common man only needs to *look* good; he doesn't need to *be* good. On the common path, you don't need strong character or an educated mind because others think for you, telling you what to wear, how to act, and how to live. There is nothing deep about you. Common is a painted mask with nothing real behind it.

But thankfully, common is not the only option. You can choose to be uncommon.

Uncommon is much more difficult. It is not always safe; it is not always smooth. An uncommon man makes waves. He is willing to stand alone, refusing to go along with the crowd, because he will not simply follow others through life.

Uncommon is hard work, too. The uncommon man has goals and dreams and is willing to do the work to achieve them. He is not afraid of sweat, of long hours of dedicated practice. He does not let mistakes sidetrack his efforts. He dusts himself off and tries again. He is not satisfied with just getting by. Being Uncommon means pushing to achieve the greatest heights possible.

But most of all, uncommon is real. The uncommon life requires strong morals and values; it focuses on the heart and mind first. An uncommon man knows that who he is on the inside is more important than how he looks on the outside. He doesn't want to look good and sound good. He wants to *be* good. And because he doesn't depend on other people to determine who he is and how he behaves, he has a swagger all his own.

He is uncommon. And it shows.

So...now which one sounds better to you? My goal, my hope, is that this book will inspire you to reach beyond the Common to find the Uncommon. To **be** uncommon.

I want you to be like the man who built his house on a foundation of stone. His buddies built their houses on sandy ground, on unstable foundations that collapsed at the first sign of difficulty, but this man's house was different. When the storms of life came, his house stood firm.[1] That is what it means to be Uncommon.

The Real Truth

I won't lie to you. Becoming uncommon is not an easy road. It'll be the hardest thing you ever do.

And why is that?

Because the fact is...you live in a very common world.

Everywhere you turn, you must deal with the common way of thinking. Big companies want you to be a mindless consumer, wasting your money on each new trend. Movies, music, TV, and advertising want you to believe that fame is the ultimate goal, that money buys happiness, and that you only have value if you have six-pack abs, designer clothes and a supermodel girlfriend.

The fact is...your world is training you to think common.

You face a constant pressure to be like everyone else... because they have chosen the common path and they want you there with them. They don't want you to outshine them, to stand for something of value, to demonstrate that there is more to you and to life than designer kicks and hip hop moguls.

The fact is...nearly everyone and everything around you is living out the common creed.

YOLO ("You Only Live Once") is the common philosophy. Who cares about helping others and committing your life to something that matters? You gotta get yours, get it today, and worry about the future when it hits you squarely between the eyes. Win at any cost. The common creed says, "Forget everyone else. I'm gonna make the most of ME."

That is how the common life works. And it surrounds you. It draws you in. The common world is pulling at you like a rip tide, and it is relentless. It's not just tough to get away...it's nearly impossible. And you will have to fight with all you've got to achieve the uncommon life.

What's Missing

But it wasn't always this way.

What is common now used to be unusual. What is uncommon today used to be the norm.

It used to be that young men were taught about hard work, respect, and working together for the greater good. It used to be that winning one for the team was better than being the all-star. It used to be that boys knew how to work, and work hard, for what they wanted. They took pride in how they dressed so that they would be known as gentlemen. They refused to satisfy every right-now desire to get something better later on. They knew how to provide for their families, how to treat a lady, how to respect their elders, how to stand up for those who needed help.

They knew all of that, and they did it. And because they did, they created a country and a generation of men who were uncommon.

But gradually, we lost our way. Since that time, the foundations of our society have shifted. Things have changed. And not for the better. common took over.

So what happened? How did we get where we are today? How did Common come to rule the world?

First, we lost our families.

At one time, the family was the foundation of everything. ALL the men–Dad, Granddad, and Uncles–worked together to help the family succeed. If Dad was struggling, his dad reminded him of how he was raised, what he had been taught. If a son needed a different perspective, an uncle provided a great sounding board. Working together, families helped boys become men and men become a nation.

But in our common world, the family is falling apart. Now, most boys do not have a dad. Instead of having generations of family members working together, nearly half the children in America will witness the breakup of their families, sometimes more than once.[2] These days, nearly 30% of children in America grow up living apart from their father.[3] For black children, the number is 60%.[4]

I know this problem firsthand. My dad was not around while I was growing up. The first real male leader I ever knew was my fifth-grade teacher, Mr. Burroughs. There were no other generations to lean on. There were no family bonds. It was me, just me, trying to figure it all out for myself. And I suspect most of you reading this book are living the same crazy life.

But we didn't just lose our families. We also lost male accountability.

Without fathers or father figures, there was no one to hold each new generation to the high standards of the uncommon path. Boys need their fathers to show them how to live, to encourage them to be men. Boys need their fathers to set the standard and then teach them the skills to reach that standard.

Without fathers to empower them to become men, boys are at a much higher risk of dropping out of school, committing crimes, and abusing drugs and alcohol.[5] They turn to gangs as a substitute for male role models. They get angry, they get sick, and they get distant. Due to the lack of a father.

Of course, mothers are important, too. We need our mothers to provide and take care of us. But their desire to love and nurture us can be counter protective. Mothers want to "fix" things for us, to shield us from the consequences of our own choices. Her child's grade is low, the coach cuts her son, the teacher hands out a detention, and in comes Mom, demanding that all be forgiven. Mothers mean well. They try to protect their kids from harm. But all they really protect their children from is...accountability.

And boys need accountability.

Without accountability, boys grow up wild, believing they should not be restricted, demanding the freedom to do as they please all the time. With no accountability, boys lose all motivation to do better, live better, be better. They will have no ambition to be uncommon men. That's why we need a return to accountability.

We lost our families. We lost accountability. But we also lost our patience.

Our common world demands instant gratification. Instead of waiting for our next paycheck to buy something, we buy it on credit right now. Commercials promise instant happiness with a simple purchase. Reality TV bombards us with endless hours of people doing crazy things, getting everything they want, and avoiding the consequences for any decision they make.

And most people want to live just like that.

We want what we want, right now, and nothing and no one can stand in our way. We get cut off in traffic and explode in anger. Someone steals money from a charity to buy a new car. Students want the A, but cheat on the exam to get it. In our world, it's all okay because it gets us what we want without the work and without the wait.

Common has cost us our families, our accountability, and our patience. And, lastly, it has cost us our schools.

Schools used to teach children to read and write and do math. Students prepared for the real world, real jobs and real life. But now, schools focus on GPA instead of values, on standardized tests instead of true learning. Instead of encouraging good grades, some schools are doing away with grades altogether. Instead of teaching common sense, schools focus on feel-good rhetoric and test scores. The common has crept in, and young men have lost yet another path to the uncommon life.

We live in a common world, without family, without accountability, without patience and without our schools. The uncommon life that used to be the norm has disappeared almost completely. But we can get it back. It *can* be done.

And it starts with you.

You can be part of the uncommon revolution. You can choose to live uncommon, and together, we can win back all that has been lost.

Living Uncommon

Gentlemen, the uncommon life is not easy, but it is absolutely vital that we walk this path. Because uncommon is the *only* path that leads to greatness.

Consider George Washington Carver.

Born to slaves in 1864, he became one of the foremost scientists and educators of his day. He worked hard and studied hard, and his research had a significant effect on American agriculture, particularly for African Americans in the South.

George Washington Carver was Uncommon. And he recognized the importance of the Uncommon life. He said, *"When you do the common things in life in an uncommon way, you will command the attention of the world."*[5]

Did you see that?

Only the Uncommon man will command the attention of the world. Only the one who stands alone, works hard, and refuses with all his being to walk the Common path will advance to a place where he can change the world.

This is your challenge. That this generation of young men would rise up and claim the uncommon path. That young men would be empowered to develop a strong foundation built on wise principles–respect for others, the value of hard work, and a willingness to sacrifice today for a reward tomorrow. That boys would decide that they *will* be their brother's keeper, that they will reach out to the weak and needy, that they will use their strength to serve.

This is the challenge. That you would join a movement of young men who are willing to do whatever it takes to break out of the mold of Common and pursue wholeheartedly the higher calling of becoming Uncommon.

It won't be easy, but it can be done. And it begins...with your NAME.

Discussion Questions

1. Living Common typically means being a follower. Do you consider yourself a leader or a follower? Why?
2. Why do you think living Uncommon takes hard work?
3. What is accountability? Why do you think a young man needs accountability to become Uncommon?
4. Is living Uncommon really possible? What do you think it would take to have that kind of life?

1. I think I am a leader because I dont copy people. And I am uncomon

2. Because being common is easy uncomon is not.

3. Because when you grow up you will forget to be uncammon.

4. Yes. It is possible and I think it is hard to live uncommon becaus to many people are common.

Chapter 2

Uncommon Identity

The First Test

I'm going to start with a basic truth about the world. This is foundational. If you miss this, you miss everything. Here it is:

*Everything about you is determined by what you **value**.*

Did you get that? Everything you do, everything you are, everything you become, is determined by what you **value**. *Everything*.

Every choice you make reveals what you value. Every decision you face will come down to what you value. Everything from how you treat people, to how you dress, to whom you marry, to where you go for lunch today is always determined by what you value.

Think about it. If you value a starting position on the football team, you spend your spare time practicing. If you value family, you hang out with them. If you value money, you find ways to get more of it. If you value celebrity, you will do whatever it takes to make sure the whole world knows your name.

And in the journey towards uncommon, what you value is the key.

You cannot become uncommon with common values. You might be able to pretend for a while. You might be able to fake it for a time. But eventually, the truth will come out. Eventually, your true values will show up. Eventually, you will begin to act and think common because your values determine everything about you.

If uncommon is your goal, you have to make sure that your values match the man you want to be. It cannot be faked. It cannot be masked. So it's not enough to talk about the outside, how to dress or how to behave. We have to start on the inside...with what you truly value.

Because the only way to become uncommon is to value what is **Uncommon**.

Valuable Things

So what is an uncommon value? Well, before we go there, let's talk about values you should avoid. Let's start with Common values. And what does a Common man value?

Simply put, Common men value Common things. For example...

- Food: They focus on what they just ate or what they plan to eat. They take pride in the variety or cost of their food. Like the California restaurant that sells a $150 hot dog.[1] No matter what it's made of, it's still a hot dog, yet Common people would put a lot of value in having tasted it.
- Alcohol: They brag about the kinds they've tasted and how much they drank before passing out at last weekend's party.
- Sex: They talk up their prowess or how many conquests they've made.
- Their Body: They're constantly sharing how much they bench press, how much weight they've gained or lost, how many crunches they can do.
- Accomplishments: They focus on their free throw percentage or how much time they've taken off their

sprints. They are consumed by what level they've beaten in *Halo* or *Call of Duty*. What they can do is all they can talk about.

· <u>Their Stuff</u>: Their TV. Their car (or dream car). Clothes, shoes, iPhones, what they spend their money on (or want to spend it on) is all that they can focus on.

Of course, these are not the only common values. But they are good examples. They represent the kinds of things that common men value. And the kinds of things those common men values are all alike in one important way.

A common value isn't really valuable at all.

The problem with anything that common men value is that *it won't last*. You won't be able to bench press that weight for the rest of your life. There's always another video game level to beat. You'll get hungry again. No matter how much time or money you spend, no matter how good it looks on the outside, it will all fade away. Common values have no staying power. They are little things. Temporary things. None of it is permanent.

To be Uncommon, you have to go a different route.

You cannot focus only on what you've done or plan to do. You have to stop chasing the shiny things advertisers dangle in front of your face and start putting value on things that last. Things that matter. The things that can be handed down to future generations.

Like your Name.

Yes, you read that correctly. To be uncommon, you have to recognize the value of your Name.

Truly Valuable

Everybody's got a name. First name, middle name, last name. Some are popular. Some are old-fashioned. Others are completely made up. Some people even have nicknames.

Obviously, having a name is not unusual. But understanding the importance of your Name is a very uncommon thing.

In our common world, a name is just a name. It is what you are called when someone wants your attention. It has no meaning or value. It can be thrown around carelessly. You can give it to anyone you want. You can behave any way you want without hurting it.

But that is the common way of thinking.

Uncommon understands that your Name *does* have value. It is a treasure worth guarding. That's why a famous proverb says: "A good name is to be chosen rather than great riches."[2]

Common values don't last. Strength fades. Wealth disappears. Stuff can never give you worth. But your Name is a treasure absolutely beyond measure. In fact, it is pretty much the most important thing about you.

The Value of a Name

Gentlemen, your name is priceless, and its value comes from its power and its potential to influence the world.

A name is powerful because it represents you. It symbolizes *who you are*.

In the past, people got this. In the past, people were careful with their names. They did not sign their names on just any dotted line. And when they did sign their names, they did it with purpose.

Like John Hancock.

The first to sign the Declaration of Independence in 1776, his signature was the largest on the page. Why? Because his Name represented his SELF. He was putting *himself* on the line. From that day on, he was a traitor; he could have been killed just because he signed his name.[3]

Your Name has that same value.

28

Your Name represents YOU. It represents who you are, all that you stand for, all that you have accomplished and will eventually do. Your Name and your Self are the same. They cannot be divided. They cannot be divorced.

But your Name is also directly tied to your reputation. Sometimes this is a good thing. Sometimes it isn't. But every time people hear a name, they immediately have an opinion, positive or negative, about that person.

Think about it. Lindsay Lohan's name brings up mental images of mug shots and drug busts. Beyonce's name is connected with power, beauty, and talent. The name of Dr. Martin Luther King, Jr., still represents gentle strength, the power of language, and the hope of a better tomorrow.

Michael Jordan's name has had uncommon staying power. He hasn't played in a basketball game in ten seasons, but after a decade, his Name still brings to mind athletic greatness; he is still the one everyone else is compared to. And even after all that time, his Name, the Jordan brand, still sells basketball shoes for Nike.

But a Name is not just powerful. It is also potentially influential. Your Name alone can create opportunities for influence — in your family, your school, your community, and your world.

Influence is the ability to affect other people's ideas and actions. A person with influence motivates others to think and act the way he wants them to. But influence doesn't just happen. People have to trust you. People have to respect you. People have to believe that you are someone worth listening to.

Only when your *name*, and your reputation, is uncommon, will people see you as exactly that kind of man. Only then will you be able to have influence in their lives.

Mr. Burroughs, my fifth grade teacher, is a great example of this. His Name stood for strength and integrity. And because he was uncommon, he was able to influence a number of young men, including me, in positive and long-lasting ways.

Oddly enough, my name is also proof of this principle. I am Tim Brown, staff member and director of sports camps for Fellowship of Christian Athletes. But there is another Tim Brown who was a Heisman Trophy winner and NFL all-star wide receiver.

Working with athletes and coaches as I do, I am sometimes asked if I am that Tim Brown. Of course, I'm not. But they ask because, with all of his accomplishments, that Tim Brown has already earned their respect. They would love to talk to him, ask his advice, and hear his stories. They hear his name and wonder if that successful player might be available to speak into their lives. His name alone opens the door to potential influence.

The same can be true for you. When your *name* represents something worthwhile, others will look to you for advice and input. You will have influence in their lives.

But, of course, the flip side is also true. If a positive, uncommon name creates influence, then a negative, common name will destroy it.

Like Lance Armstrong. He was long considered a superior athlete and philanthropist. But his admission of doping changed everything. When it was revealed that he had cheated and then lied about it for years, he lost his reputation, both in the sport of racing and in his Livestrong foundation. His Name lost its power and its influence.

Your name can be Common or Uncommon. It can be influential, or it can be a punchline. So the only question that remains is...what does *your* Name say about you?

Protect your Name

Thankfully, you can avoid Lance Armstrong's mistake. Your Name can have power. It can open doors of influence for you.

But only if you protect it.

Above all other things, you must protect your Name. It is your responsibility. No one can protect it for you. You have to recognize its value and guard that value, no matter the cost.

And keep in mind...everything you do either adds value to your Name or takes it away. There is no such thing as an act or word that doesn't matter. When it comes to protecting your Name, **nothing** you do is neutral.

Nike gets this idea. Here is a company that is highly protective of its Name. They hire the best and biggest athletes to be their representatives, but if any of those athletes' actions or words detract from the value of Nike's name, their contracts are ended. Immediately.

That's what happened to Michael Vick. In 2007, he was a Nike spokesman with a line of shoes and shirts bearing his name. But when he was charged with dogfighting, Nike suspended his contract and later ended it altogether.[4] Since then, they've also cut ties with Lance Armstrong[5] and Oscar Pistorius[6] because of their negative actions.

Just like Nike, you must take the protection of your Name seriously. You must make sure that its value is always positive. That you are building it up, and never tearing it down. You must act and speak only in ways that add value to your name. It is too important to do less.

So how do you protect your name?

THINK. Don't just react to circumstances. Make intentional decisions. Choose your words carefully because they can come back to haunt you. Consider the consequences of your actions because foolish, dangerous or illegal behavior will decrease the value and influence of your Name. Learn to act responsibly, speak carefully, and think fully.

How do you protect your name?

WAIT. Don't rush into decisions. Don't let your buddies push you into stupid stunts. Don't demand instant gratification. It is always wise to take your time and not just live for the moment. Learn to take a long view; live with your future in mind.

You must make sure that your behavior adds value to your name, creating for your Name a power and influence that will last.

Your Name, Your Legacy

Protecting your name is not easy. But it must be done. For yourself and for your future.

Yes, your Name can give you power and influence. But that is only part of the picture. Even more importantly, your Name has value because it is part of something bigger than just you alone. It has lasting worth because you pass it on to the next generation. Your Name is a **legacy**.

Simply put, your Name is the name of a Nation.

Every man has the chance to build a Nation on his name. To do this, he accepts the legacy of his Name from those who came before him. He accepts the challenge to lead his generation of the Nation, and then, having added value to that Name, he passes it on to the young men who will carry the Name after him.

This kind of Nation-building has almost disappeared in our individualistic culture. Boys "become" men at 18. In one moment, they are cut loose from the authority of their families. And at the same time, they are expected to be able to act like adults, making good decisions and not acting like kids anymore.

Not surprisingly, most young men do not make that leap successfully. Without anyone to model and encourage uncommon behavior, most young men become common. They behave poorly, make bad decisions, and destroy the value of their Name, leaving nothing to pass on to those who come after them.

But it can be done. It is possible to recognize the value of a Name and from it build a long-lasting Nation of strong and influential men.

Jewish families do this kind of Nation-building very well. At thirteen, each Jewish boy becomes Bar Mitzvah; he reaches the age of obligation. From that point on, he is considered a man, fully responsible for his actions and his commitment to keeping the Jewish commandments.[7]

But at 13, he is not cut loose to find his own way. He continues to live with his family, being trained by his father and other Jewish leaders to live out the commitment he made at his thirteenth birthday. By the time he leaves his father's authority, he has a Name of great worth. He has developed the ability to protect his Name and to train up the next generation behind him as well.

That is the kind of Nation that every man *can* build from his Name. A Nation of influence and power. A Nation of strong men who will lead their families and communities. An uncommon Nation.

Family Legacies

Strong Nations like these do exist.

Take the Kennedy family. For over a hundred years, the Kennedys have influenced American life. John F. Kennedy was President of the United States. Robert Kennedy was Attorney General. Ted Kennedy was a Congressman for almost 50 years. Members of this family have served as governors, senators, representatives, and ambassadors. They have been journalists, lawyers, philanthropists and everyday citizens who have played a major role in what our country has become.[8]

The Kennedy name has value. The Kennedy Nation is Uncommon.

Or consider the Manning family. In two generations, the Manning family has produced three NFL quarterbacks.

Archie Manning played in the NFL for thirteen seasons. Peyton and Eli Manning, Archie's sons, have added to the value of the Manning name by excelling as quarterbacks, leading their teams to Super Bowl victories and earning MVP honors for themselves.[9]

The Manning name has value. The Manning Nation is Uncommon.

We call these Nations dynasties. These families that produce influential, successful men and women generation after generation. The Earnhardt family. The Ripken family. The Griffey family. Just mention the *NAME*, and everyone remembers the achievements and the legacies. Everyone recognizes the Nation that was created when men accepted the challenge to be uncommon and passed on uncommon values to the sons who came after them.

The Challenge

Gentlemen, the same can be true for you. You can choose, today, to create a Nation for your Name.

That is what I did. My nation is the Brown Nation. My sons are part of my Nation. We share the Brown Name, and we hold it in high esteem because it means something. Great Brown men before us helped to build the Name, and we are committed to adding value to it.

The Brown Nation values education, family togetherness, love, and compassion for others. We intentionally live in such a way that we live out these values. The Brown Nation desires a legacy of encouraging others to be successful through hard work and lifting others up so that they, too, can achieve their dreams. In the Brown Nation, we stand for truth even if we have to stand alone. We have chosen to be uncommon because common does not work in our Nation.

That is my Nation. That is who I am, who my sons are. They understand the value of this Nation, and they strive to add value to the legacy that I have started for them.

But such a Nation is not a given. And that is the challenge I make to you.

I challenge you to choose an uncommon identity, to create an uncommon Nation. Your Nation is not my Nation. Your values do not have to be the same as mine. But I challenge you to accept that you are part of the Nation of your Name. It was handed to you by the men who came before you. You are reaping the benefits of great men who paved the way for your success.

Now it is time for you to do the same.

You must put away the common things you have stood for and lived for and, instead, begin to pursue the Name and the Nation that you alone can create. It is time for you to pursue an *uncommon* identity, to decide that your Name will be valuable and to protect it at all costs. It is time for you to accept the challenge of creating a Nation that stands for ideas and values that have lasting significance.

It is time for you to choose an *uncommon* identity. Not a mask to wear in order to impress people, but a real change of heart that will affect everything about who you are and how you live.

And it all begins with your Swagger...

Discussion Questions

1. Do you think the list of Common values is a good list? Which of those things have you heard people say? What else might you add to the list?
2. Do you agree that your Name is the most important thing about you?
3. What can you do to protect your name? What should you avoid doing?
4. We talked about building a Nation on your Name. What values would you want your Nation to stand for? How can you begin now to add Value to your Nation?

Chapter 3

Uncommon Swagg

Your Swagger Style

E very man is known for his swagger.
Swagger is how you present yourself to the world. It's about how you act and react. It's your walk, your talk, your style. And it is a good thing. As John Calipari, head coach of the UK men's basketball team, said, "The best teams I've had had a little bit of a swagger."[1]

But swagger is not what most people think it is.

Most men spend a lot of time and money trying to prove they have swagger. They try to project an attitude of style and sophistication. But that's the problem. It's just an attitude. It isn't real.

Like we said in the last chapter, you can only fake who you are for so long. Eventually your true identity will reveal itself. Someone with common values will eventually live out those values. Only an uncommon man will display uncommon values and live out an uncommon identity.

Swagger is the same. Your swagger will be the first place that your true identity shows up. Common or Uncommon, your swagger will display exactly what kind of a man you are.

Faking your Swagger

So what does common swagg look like?

Common swagg is fake. It's only skin-deep. It's a twisted version of true swagger, and it is anything but real.

Common swagg is a false front, a mask men use to hide who they really are. This swagger is all about image. It's about creating a look, a disguise. The focus is on the outside with little concern for anything underneath, and the goal is to be seen a certain way, to get a certain kind of treatment.

It's like the kicker on the eighth-grade football team finding a Varsity letter jacket somewhere and wearing it to school the next day.

He might try to hang out with the senior quarterback and his buddies; he might try to walk like them, talk like them, act like them. But it wouldn't last. The jacket alone is not enough to change his true identity. He's still just an eighth grader, and the truth would quickly come out.

Common swagger works the same way. It's the disguise a lot of guys wear. They think it makes them cool, makes them look like a man. But it doesn't. Like an eighth grader trying to pull off a Varsity jacket, this kind of swagger is always the mark of a pretender.

It's also the mark of an arrogant man.[2] A man with false swagger is overbearing to everyone around him. He is cocky. He is a jerk. The guy with this attitude treats other people badly. He is disrespectful and rude.

Think Kanye West. He has a history of tantrums and angry rants, culminating most recently in his rude behavior to Taylor Swift at the VMA awards in 2009.[3] Though he typically apologizes for his outbursts, the fact is, his actions reveal what lies under his superstar facade. Regardless of what you think of his music, his attitude is totally arrogant.

But on top of being fake, Common swagger also drives people away.

Real swagger is attractive; it brings people toward you. But false swagger pushes people away. As one article put it, the man with common swagg "thinks and acts as if he is superior to others, in turn, causing others to think badly of him and dislike him."[4]

Celebrities can often behave this way. Justin Bieber. Chris Brown. Nicki Minaj. Charlie Sheen. They seem to be full of themselves, behaving poorly and treating people badly. And because of their attitudes, people don't like them. They have swagger, but it doesn't create a positive or uncommon reputation. Their swagger does just the opposite. They are disliked.

I've seen athletes behave this way, too. They take advantage of people in a negative and arrogant way, not realizing the impact it has on them and others. They accept gifts, break the rules, and use their position to get what they want. They are cocky and unkind, and the swagger they present eventually turns away even their biggest fans.

Finding True Swagger

But Common swagger is not the only option. Swagger doesn't have to be an offensive and obnoxious disguise.

Instead, your swagger can move you forward and have a positive effect on your life, your friends, and your future. Your style can help you to influence others and give you an air of authority. People will sense your confidence and will trust what you have to say.

In other words, you can have uncommon Swagg.

Uncommon Swagg is true swagger. This attitude isn't cocky or rude. Uncommon Swagg lifts people up and influences them in a positive way. It is a humble attitude. A man with Uncommon Swagg doesn't expect to be treated as if he's special, but believes that he is blessed to be a blessing to others.

Even more, uncommon Swagg is real. It's deep, more than just outward appearance. It is not a mask to cover up a bad attitude. It comes from the inside, from true values and a true identity. A man with uncommon Swagg wants the world to see more than his clothes or kicks. Instead of focusing on image alone (the outward appearance), uncommon swagger has true I.M.A.G.E. That means he wants others to

Imagine
Me
A
Gentleman of
Excellence.

An Uncommon man wants to be a Gentleman of Excellence. But what does that look like?

First, true swagger does consider the outward appearance. A true gentleman cares about his clothes, but does not let them define him. He is well-groomed and stylish, but he does not need to follow every trend, every fad. He knows his style affects his influence and reputation with others, so he creates a personal flair that is tasteful, not offensive.[5] Simply put, he takes his appearance into account, but he is not consumed by it.

Style is important, but it's only one piece of the puzzle. As one celebrity stylist noted, true swagger is "Manners + Confidence + Style."[6] In other words, to have true swagger, you have to look good on the inside as well as the outside.

A Gentlemen of Excellence knows that real swagger comes from the heart, not a store. A man with uncommon Swagg is confident without being arrogant (confidence). He knows who he is and is not threatened by other people; he is sure of himself, seeing no need to bend to peer pressure. But he also focuses on making those around him feel at ease (manners). He is gracious even in high-pressure or difficult situations. He handles himself with dignity and an even temper.

He is a true Gentleman.

Uncommon Spirit

Most importantly, though, a Gentleman of Excellence understands that his Swagg is always tied directly to his Spirit. If a man's Spirit is immature, offensive or corrupt, his swagger will be the same. But a Gentleman of Excellence will have an uncommon Spirit, marked by three particular characteristics.[7]

1. A Spirit of Desire

To be uncommon, to be a true Gentleman, a young man must have a vision for his future. Instead of aimlessly wandering through life, a spirit of desire means knowing what you want and being willing to work, and work hard, to reach that goal.

This Spirit can show up in many different areas, but above all else, I want to challenge every young man to pursue a Desire for education. I am convinced that one of the best expressions of uncommon Swagg is to have initials that mean something following your name — B.A., M.B.A., Ph.D., L.S.W., to name a few.

Nothing in life will empower you like a good education. My mother instilled this truth in me as a very young man. She would remind me that education is the one thing that no one can take away from you. It is yours forever, a treasure that will enable you to succeed in any other area you pursue.

And she was absolutely right.

That is why, when I taught fifth grade, I required my students to read *Gifted Hands* in the summer before they entered my class. This book is the story of Ben Carson, an inner city boy who became an innovative and influential doctor. He struggled in school, but his mother, though undereducated herself, pushed him to read and to believe in himself. Then, after fifth grade, things began to change for him. Carson went from being a poor student to being an honors student. He graduated and attended Yale medical school. As a doctor, he eventually became the director of pediatric neurosurgery at Johns Hopkins at age 33, and he became famous for his work separating conjoined twins.

Dr. Ben Carson was an uncommon man who had a Spirit of Desire for education, and his education enabled him to achieve amazing feats.

The same can be true for you.

There was a sign in my junior high school that read "Knowledge is power." I have learned that without wisdom knowledge is useless. Your education is the most powerful tool available to help you become truly uncommon. But you have to Desire it. You have to pursue it. Your middle school and high school years will provide unparalleled opportunities to get as much knowledge as you can. Do not waste them.

Get knowledge. Be an educated man because that knowledge will empower you to achieve great things and to have great influence. It will empower you to become the provider and leader of your family in the future. And it will make you a model for your future children, a clear example of how to value education at any age.

The Desire for a good education is a key element of what the Brown Nation stands for. I have always stressed the importance of education to my sons. My wife and I set a goal for them that we would help them get a Masters degree, and we have done that. But we have also challenged them to take the importance of education to the next level by ensuring that their children, our grandchildren, have the opportunity to receive a Ph.D. if they desire it.

A Spirit of Desire means you dream big.

I challenge you to make a plan for your life, for your education, no matter how unrealistic it might seem to other people. Decide, today, that you are going to graduate, go to college, get an advanced degree. Decide, today, that you will not be stopped by financial questions or other people's doubts. Make your education a priority and pursue it with all your heart. This is the best way to live out the Spirit of Desire.

2. *A Spirit of Kindness*

An extensive education without a well-developed heart leads only to arrogance. A Gentleman of Excellence balances his Spirit of Desire with a heart that is Kind. He learns and uses proper etiquette and manners. He shows respect for others by saying "please" and "thank you."[8] He holds doors, tips well, looks people in the eye, offers to assist those who need help, and seeks to treat each person they meet like a friend.

A Spirit of Kindness means that you realize that you **are** your brother's keeper. You recognize your responsibility for the people around you. And you choose, as much as possible, to follow life's golden rule: "Do unto others as you would have them do to you."[9]

3. *A Spirit of Justice*

Finally, a true Gentleman balances his view of himself and his view of the world. Men with false swagger are self-absorbed, seeing only themselves and what they want. But a man with uncommon Swagg seeks more than just his own good. He seeks a Spirit of Justice.

A Spirit of Justice is the opposite of an attitude of entitlement. It means you understand that the world does not, in fact, owe you anything. Instead, it means taking the many blessings you have and using those resources to help others. Justice means attempting, as much as you are able, to right the wrongs. It means being committed to the truth, defending the weak, protecting the poor. A just person does what is right.

A Spirit of Justice means having some backbone and choosing to be counted in the areas of life that truly matter. A Gentleman of Excellence will not back down when pressured by friends to do wrong or to compromise. Instead, he is willing to sacrifice his own comfort to relieve the suffering of others; he meets their needs in any way that he can.

Swagger is always determined by Spirit. A true Gentleman will pursue a Spirit of Desire, of Kindness, and of Justice because those three qualities will make sure that his Swagg is real. Those three qualities will ensure that he becomes a leader wherever he goes, influencing others and building them up to become true gentlemen as well.

The IT Factor

A true Gentlemen will always have Uncommon Swagg. To put it another way, he will have the "It factor."

The "It factor" is an "indefinable something that makes someone special."[10] It's known as Court Presence in sports. When the game is close, and it is crunch time, you want the guy who has "it" to have the ball so he can take the shot or make the game-changing play.

But this quality can show up anywhere. It's the "X Factor" for singers or movie stars. It's the *something* the manager is looking for when you sit down for a job interview. It's the quality that earns that lucky guy a date with the *real* good girl–the one you have to work hard for and who's turned down all the other guys.

But no matter where it shows up, every guy wants to be the one who has "it." Everybody wants to be the guy with the intangibles, the things you can't see on the outside, but that must be there to get the win, get the role, get the girl, get the job. People know who has Uncommon Swagger, and deep down, they want what he has.

But wanting it is not enough to make it happen.

It has to start from the right place, from your heart. You have to first have an Uncommon identity. You cannot fake it. And then you have to work hard for it. True swagger is earned over time. It is formed by experience, by repeatedly making the right decisions, the hard decisions, and pursuing your Nation and your education without letting up.[11]

You can live Uncommon. You can develop Uncommon Swagg. You can become the one who leads and influences those around him, the one that others follow.

But it won't be easy. And it will never happen unless you first find Uncommon friends...

Discussion Questions

1. What is swagger? Give examples of people you think have swagger?
2. IMAGE stands for "Imagine me a Gentleman of Excellence." What do you think a Gentleman of Excellence looks like?
3. What are 2 goals you can set for yourself in the area of education? What would it take for you to reach those goals?
4. Why is it important for a Gentleman of Excellence to have a Spirit of Desire? Of Kindness? Of Justice? What would each of these look like in your life right now?

1. I think the whole boys wont be boys group has swagger.

2. He looks good on the inside and the outside.

3. my times tables, division, and subtraction

4. Greatful, happy, and helpaul

Chapter 4

Uncommon Friends

The Big Picture

So let's recap.
To become Uncommon, you have to have uncommon values. You have to accept the challenge to embrace an uncommon identity and to build the Nation of your Name. When you accept that challenge, your life begins to change. You get a new swagger.

Your swagger will reveal to anyone watching you just how uncommon you really are because, instead of settling for a cheap disguise, your uncommon Swagg will mark you as a Gentleman of Excellence who values education and treats others well.

That's the plan. That's the goal. BUT. All of that progress can come to a screeching halt if you don't also have Uncommon friends.

That's right...just as you can't be uncommon with common values, you can't be uncommon with common friends.

To Friend or Not To Friend

Unfortunately, common friends are, well...common. Most of your friendships will fall into this category.

In basic terms, a friend is simply "a person known well to another and regarded with liking, affection and loyalty; an acquaintance or associate, a supporter."[1]

This is a pretty broad definition. And that's okay. Because just about anybody *can* be your friend. A good friendship isn't determined by how you met or whether you both like to play *Call of Duty*. What is important is whether or not your friendships are uncommon.

So how will you know what kind of friends you have? Well, common "friends" show up in one of two ways.

First, common friends can be fakes. People who are nice to your face and then stab you in the back. These "friends" are users. They want something from you. They hit you up for money, your science notes, or a ride to the game, but they offer nothing in return. They are emotionally draining, even damaging. They aren't true friends.

And, unfortunately, any friend can turn out to be fake. The kid you've known since second grade might suddenly dump you for a new group of friends. Out of nowhere, the friend who's had your back all year stabs it instead. False friends don't always look bad at first, but when they turn on you, your best bet is simply to walk away. They have chosen a common path, and if you stay connected to them, they will keep you from uncommon.

But most of your common friends won't be ones who betray you. More often than not, they're the ones you "talk" to every day...online.

Facebook, Instagram and Twitter. Snapchat, Kik or Vine. The goal of these apps is to create a following, to have as many people as possible check out your site even one time. Yes, you know some of them IRL (*in real life*, for any adults reading this). But most of them are just names. They are not friends. And that makes them common.

Now, I'm not saying that you should avoid social networking completely. That isn't going to happen, but you do need to pay attention to the quality of your online relationships. The sheer number of online "friends" we have should tip us off to just how fake these "friendships" are. Most people have hundreds or thousands of friends on online sites. I saw one high school football player who had over four thousand friends on Facebook.

Four thousand? That's not friendship. It is impossible to have real relationships with that many so-called friends. It would take you almost two weeks (day *and* night) to greet all four thousand friends for just five minutes at a time...that's not friendship!

Common thinking says that the important thing is having more "friends" than anyone else. But numbers do not equal connections. And that is the problem. We are so consumed with keeping up with our online reality that we often ignore the people in the very same room with us while we text, chat, or send pics online.

Of course, online relationships do have value. They do. But we must stop pretending that our online activity is about real relationship. They keep us on top of each new viral video. But they don't meet any real social and emotional needs. They are names on a news feed. They are not friends.

Prioritizing online "friends" is common. And it's flawed big-time. It is a substitute for the real thing. To be Uncommon, this "normal" will never work. To choose an uncommon life, you have to take part in an entirely different reality.

You must invest in real friendships.

The Power of Friends

Uncommon friendships are, not surprisingly, uncommon. They don't happen often. You will not have hundreds or thousands of uncommon friends. You might have five. You might only have one. But you must begin to cultivate this kind of support system. You cannot become uncommon without it.

So where do you begin? You begin with three basic truths.

1. Real friends are essential, not optional.

Some of you prefer to be a Lone Ranger. You don't need friends. You don't want friends. They get in the way. They take more than they give. They add drama that you just don't need.

But you are wrong.

Friends are not optional. We need them. Yes, some friends complicate our lives. But we still need them. We need true friends. We need people who are part of our lives in a real and personal way.

And why do we need friends? Because of what they do for us.

Real friends speak truth to us.

Most people don't want anyone to say the hard stuff to them. They don't want bad news. They don't want people to bring them down. They don't want anyone to make them stop and think; they want "friends" who just go with the flow and have a good time.

But those are not the people you need to be with. Those are not real friends.

True friends tell you when you've screwed up. They call you out for the mistakes you make. They tell you to think before you do something stupid, something you'll regret. They stand up to you, and they want you to stand up to them in return.

Telling us the truth, even when it hurts, is the mark of a genuine friend. As one proverb says, "Wounds from a friend are better than many kisses from an enemy."[2] Someone who only tells us how great we are, who tells us only what we want to hear, is not a friend. That person is, in fact, an enemy. He isn't looking out for you. He is looking out for himself.

Real friends aren't afraid to say what needs to be said. Even if we don't like it. Even when we don't want to hear it. Someone who makes us feel bad for a few minutes to protect us from greater harm is a true friend. Find that person and stick with him. He is uncommon.

Also, real friends make us better people.

False friends only care about themselves. They use us and drop us when we no longer serve their purposes.

But a true friend builds us up. They push us to grow and help us become the people we want to be. "As iron sharpens iron, a friend sharpens a friend."[3] A blade must be sharp to work as it should, but the only way to keep it sharp is to rub it against a sharpening tool.

That's how a good friend works, too.

By holding us to higher standards, asking the tough questions, encouraging us to live more generous and thoughtful lives, true friends act like a sharpening tool, honing us so that we can live up to our full potential as people and as friends.

Finally, real friends keep us connected — to ourselves and to others.

Too many people believe that online connections are enough. But it just doesn't work that way. Real friends want to be with us, in person. They keep us connected and remind us that we are not alone.

Friends laugh with us about nothing. They help us get over the loss of a girlfriend, our cell phone, or a Friday night football game. They remind us of the good things around us and point out the ways we can make our world a better place. They keep us from being totally consumed with our own little lives; genuine friends help us see past ourselves to the people and places around us.

That is why we need true friends: they speak truth, they make us better, they keep us connected. And that is why true friendship is very Uncommon. It won't just happen. It must be created. Which brings us to the second basic truth.

2. Friendships must be cultivated; they're not automatic.

Finding real friends doesn't just happen. It is work to find good friends, and it requires more work to create uncommon relationships, ones that bring out the best in both of you.

That's why Facebook friends just aren't enough. A real friend cannot be replaced by chats or tweets. He can't be hidden behind a profile pic or a screen shot. You do not get true friendship in 140 characters or less. You need more than that.

You need real people that you see and talk to on a regular basis. They have to be involved in your life. We all need our friends to be present, close enough that they can put an arm around us, speak to us, or give us a friendly nudge.

And that kind of involvement takes time. And effort. And intention.

As Thomas Wilson said, "Friendship is to be purchased only by friendship. A man may have authority over others, but he can never have their heart but by giving his own."[4]

True friends go out of their way to make time for each other. They work on their relationship, intentionally building each other up and purposely spending time with each other. That means that no matter how busy your schedule or how many things you have going on, you have to reserve time to talk to your friends.

And they have to do the same thing for you. If he doesn't answer your calls or texts, if there is serious doubt that he'll ever respond to a voicemail...you might need to consider whether he is a true friend.

Genuine friends are essential to our development. Real friendships require time and effort to maintain. But there is a third basic truth that you must also understand: a friend is a powerful influence.

3. Friends impact our lives; they're not neutral.

Those closest to us will rub off on us. They change us. They impact our choices and our behavior. Eventually, we will start to look like, act like, think like them. We will emulate them—copy them, follow their lead. Our friends will make a difference in our lives.

That's what was meant by the phrase, "Associate yourself with people of good quality, for it is better to be alone than in bad company."[5] Another proverb put it this way: "Bad company corrupts good character."[6]

Eventually, our friends will dictate the positions we take. Their morals become our morals. What they think and believe will start to sound better all the time. Their convictions and character (or lack thereof) eventually become ours, too. And no matter how set you are on being uncommon, if your crowd is common, you will eventually be common, too.

That's why one proverb says: "Whoever walks with the wise becomes wise, but the companion of fools will suffer harm."[7] Uncommon men recognize that the people we hang with do affect us. If we choose wise friends, they will help us become wise, too. But we cannot rub shoulders with fools and not be tainted by their foolishness.

So, remember these three principles. Friends are essential. True friendships require effort. And friends have power. Who we let into our lives influences who we become.

Now, Gentlemen, it's time to get personal.

Pegging your P.E.E.R.S.

Think, right now, about your five closest friends. Go ahead. Write their names in the margin. Got your list? Good. Now let me ask you one question.

Is your crowd the Right Crowd or the Wrong Crowd?

It's pretty easy to tell. Think about it this way: *Wrong P.E.E.R.S.* are **P**eople **E**ncouraging **E**rrors, **R**udeness, **S**tupidity.

If your five closest friends are pulling you down; if they get in trouble and get you in trouble, too; if they are rude and disrespectful to authority, their mothers, your mother, teachers, the ladies, or somebody who doesn't hang in your group; if they are known for bad choices, bad humor, bad attitudes, bad behavior...then Gentlemen, they are the Wrong Crowd.

But there is another option. It is possible that your friends are the *Right P.E.E.R.S.* They are **P**eople **E**ncouraging **E**xcellence, **R**espect, **S**uccess.

The Right Crowd are the people who build up; they don't tear down. They do the very best they can. They respect those around them. They are focused on success, and they want you to succeed, too. That is the Right Crowd.

The Right Crowd are true friends. They are the real deal. And they will be known for four powerful behaviors.

- They help, not hurt, your chances of achieving your dreams and goals. These are the guys you have history with. They have been with you through your successes and failures. They know your dreams, and they will help to keep you focused on achieving those dreams.
- You respect each other. It may not have started out that way. These guys may have been the least likely crew for you to be hanging with. But over time, you developed a respect for each other. Yes, you had differences, but as you got to know each other, you found out that you all had the same goals and objectives in life. And from that respect grew friendship.
- They stick with you. As someone once said, "Never travel with a friend who deserts you at the approach of danger."[8] At some point, trouble will come, and in that moment, you will get a very clear picture of who your real friends are. Uncommon friends will not bail when it's crunch time. When the rubber meets the road, they will be there. When the time comes, they will stand by your side.
- They are committed to accountability and integrity. These are the guys who are willing to "call you out" when you are doing something wrong or about to do

something wrong. These guys keep you grounded. They will always remind you of who you are and who you represent. And they will do whatever it takes to get you out of a situation that will lead you into trouble.

So, with all that in mind, look again at that list of five friends that you wrote in the margin. Stop and consider those names. Remember that a Name embodies the reputation of the man who carries it. And ask yourself...What do those names say about those guys?

Are they the Right Crowd? Or the Wrong one?

If they are true friends, congratulations! You are walking the uncommon path in this area. But if not–if even one of the five that you listed is a part of the Wrong Crowd–then you need to begin, right now, to distance yourself from him and replace his influence with a person or a group who will help you towards becoming uncommon.

Picking your Peers

Of course, I do realize that is easier said than done.

Your friends are part of who you are. You probably can't just break ties with them tomorrow, no questions asked, no consequences. But you can refuse to give them space in your closest group of friends anymore. If one or more of your top five is pulling you down the road of foolishness and common thinking, you need to start, today, to limit the influence they have on your life.

At the same time, you also need to start seeking out uncommon friendships. It's not enough to reduce the negative influence. You have to replace that negativity with positive influence.

So...how do you do find the Right friends?

- Smile–Lighten up. You don't have to act tough all the time. Learn to be a friendly person, someone who smiles and knows how to enjoy life.

- Listen–Let others talk about themselves, then respond. If you can, wait five seconds before you start talking. Give yourself time to really think about what they've said. And when someone else is talking, don't be thinking ahead about what you are going to say. Give that person your ear and your thoughts. It shows wisdom to talk less and listen more. As one proverbs says, "A truly wise person uses few words; a person with understanding is even-tempered. Even fools are thought to be wise when they keep silent; when they keep their mouths shut, they seem intelligent."[9]

- Be Dependable–If you make a commitment, keep it. If you promise to be somewhere, get there. If you are scheduled to work, show up. In every situation, show yourself trustworthy. Be there for others during the good and bad. Anyone can be there for the fun times, but only a friend will be there when things get tough. Keep in mind this saying, "There are 'friends' who destroy each other, but a real friend sticks closer than a brother."[10]

- Keep Your Word–"Good people are guided by their honesty; treacherous people are destroyed by their dishonesty."[11] If you say you are going to do something, do it. You won't always want to. Do it anyway. If you can't keep a promise, then don't make it in the first place. It's better to under-promise and over-achieve than to over-promise and fail to deliver. You are never too young to understand that a good man is only as good as his word. If you say you are going to do something, DO IT.

- Help Others Succeed–Be others-minded. Ask yourself, "How can I help this person? Then do what you can to assist them. Be the guy that others know will give them good advice and will help them find the right way to do something. Help keep each other on the right path.

I had a friend through Middle School who was a great example of a Right friend. Fred and his older brother were being raised by his dad, and Fred was the most respectful and well-mannered guy I knew. His dad would let me hang out with the family. Fred was a true friend who allowed me to benefit from his family and treated me like another brother. Though we drifted apart in high school, his willingness to let me be myself and share his family is something I will always remember.

I have talked to a lot of young men about what keeps them from getting distracted so they can stay on the right path. They all tell me the same thing. "Mr. Brown, I choose the right company to keep."

These guys have it figured out. They hang with other guys who are going the same direction as they are, guys who are also trying to graduate, go to college, and get a scholarship. They know the only way to get there is to be *uncommon* and be with *uncommon* guys. These guys remind me that uncommon friendships are hard to find, and the group is small, but they know it will be well worth it in the end.

Uncommon Friends

We can no longer be content with the fake friends that surround us in life and online. Instead, we must seek out uncommon friends.

Uncommon friendships are not easy. They are not pain-free. They can be very messy. But if you want to become uncommon, then you must pursue this kind of friend. Your friends will define who you are. They will influence what you think, how you behave, who you become.

Your friends, more than almost any other influence, will determine your character...and that is where we go next.

Discussion Questions

1. Do you consider yourself a true friend? Why or why not?
2. Are friends really as influential as the chapter claimed? Is peer pressure really a big problem?
3. What are the top three qualities that you look for in a friend?
4. Make a list of your top five friends. Are they good PEERS or bad PEERS? How do you know?

1. Because. I am kind and play with my friends.
2. yes. Becuse you need friends.
3. kind, careful, and honest
4. Shawn, Jayden, mason, Julen, and montrell

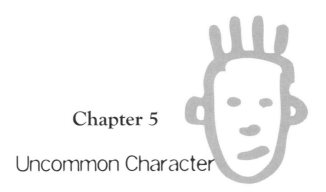

Chapter 5

Uncommon Character

Playing it Straight

U ncommon character cannot be faked.
Like your swagger and your friends, your character is a reflection of just how uncommon you are. When it's crunch time, no matter how good your disguise, who you really are is what will show through. Common or Uncommon, in the heat of the moment, your true character will be revealed.

So the question is, "How Uncommon is your character?"
There is one way to find out.

Imagine that you are playing a basketball game for your high school team. The game is almost over, the score is close, say 54-51, and your team is ahead. With just seconds to go, the ball gets loose. It ends up out of bounds, and your team is awarded the ball.

BUT. It touched your hand before rolling off the court.

No one else saw it happen. The ref missed the contact. The only person in the gym who knows what happened is you. You know that you touched the ball and the other team should have possession.

So...what do you do?[1]

Do you rat on yourself, turn the ball over to the other team and risk them hitting a 3-pointer to send the game into overtime? Or do you just keep your mouth shut and let play resume with your team in control of the ball?

Got your answer? Know which choice you would make? Good.

Because with that answer, you've just discovered whether or not you already have uncommon character.

Character Defined

There are a lot of ways to define character.

There's the dictionary definition: "the combination of traits and qualities distinguishing the individual nature of a person or thing" or "moral force; integrity."[2]

There are practical definitions like "the quality of being honest and morally upright."[3]

And there are catchy definitions, too. J.C. Watts, an African-American Congressman, once said, "Character is doing the right thing when nobody is looking."[4]

But however you define character, you have to understand exactly what character is.

Simply put, your character is the sum total of you who are. **That** is why it is so important. It's your heart. It is the culmination of all of your choices, good or bad. It is the fundamental quality of your life, the foundation of all your actions and attitudes.

Character can be good or bad. It is created as you apply your thoughts and morals and ideals to real life. Here is how one famous proverb describes it:

Watch your thoughts, they become words;
Watch your words, they become actions;
Watch your actions, they become habits;
Watch your habits, they become character;
Watch your character, for it becomes your destiny.[5]

Your character is going to determine your destiny. That's why you must develop uncommon character. You need to put away the attitudes and ideas that lead to bad decisions and begin to adopt the habits that will build within you the good qualities that mark you as Uncommon.

There are three primary characteristics of a man of character.

1. Honesty

A man of character always tells the truth. No matter the cost. No matter the audience. No matter what. As one writer put it, having character means "being honest to a fault."[6]

An honest person speaks the truth. He will not lie. He will not say things that are not true. And just as important, he will not leave out things that are true. People will only trust you when they know they can believe what you say, and the more you tell the truth, the more they will trust you.

So what does this mean practically? It means, when in doubt, tell the truth. To yourself. To your parents. To your teachers. To your friends. To authority figures. To your kid sister. To the guy who owns the convenience store. When you aren't sure what to say, tell the truth.

It will mark you as a man of character.

2. Integrity

Honesty is about what we say (or don't say). Integrity is about what we do (or don't do).

A man of character does the right thing, all the time. Integrity means that you behave morally and ethically in every situation. You choose the high road. You put others first. You don't steal or cheat or push around the kid who's smaller than you. You give. You keep your commitments. You treat everyone with respect.[7]

Integrity always marks a man of character.

3. Incorruptible Character

Living a life of consistent honesty and consistent integrity is hard. Nearly impossible, in fact. But that's why this final quality is all the more important.

A man of character is incorruptible. He is not-corruptible.

Corruption is the breakdown or decay of something that was whole. And it definitely applies in the area of character.

We often see corruption in politics, in business, and in sports. In each situation, a person trades his character for something he wants. A senator sells his vote for campaign money. The salesman sells a faulty product, knowing its flaws. A player throws a game or bets on his team or dopes to win a race.

Obviously, this is corruption. This is common character.

But it does not happen overnight. It happens when, little by little, a person's decisions and attitudes shifted away from good character towards bad. He didn't mean to sell out or cheat or lie. But there he is...corrupted.

To be incorruptible is to refuse to give in to that gradual slide away from good character.

Being incorruptible means being on guard against the influence of others. True character is a threat to those who don't have it. Common men will stop at almost nothing to ruin good character. At every turn, someone will be working to corrupt the uncommon man.

But no matter what those around him are saying or doing, the uncommon man refuses to sacrifice his character for things that don't last. He refuses to give in to the pressure to tell the "little lie," to look the other way while others cheat, to cut out of work even 10 minutes early. A man of character will not be changed. He will not be influenced. He will continue to speak the truth and do the right thing.

Because that is what it means to be incorruptible. That is what it means to be *uncommon*.

Lights, Camera, Action

So of course, good character sounds great. It should be something everyone wants. And...they do. Really, most people do want to have good character. But let's be honest here. Developing good character is hard.

It is hard work to tell the truth *all the time*. To do the right thing *all the time*. To withstand negative influences *all the time*. Having uncommon character is tough.

So most people just fake it. Instead of being a true man of character, most guys become "Care-Actors."

A Care-Actor *acts like* he has character. He knows the right thing to do, but he actually does the opposite...especially when no one else is looking. And there is the key.

Think about it this way: a buddy who is willing to pull a stupid prank as long as no one takes pictures or posts about it online...he is a Care-Actor. He is more concerned with perception than being real. He was willing to do the stupid prank. His only concern was whether someone might find out.

Care-Actors always play a role. As long as someone is watching, a Care-Actor wears the mask. But the second he is alone, his real self comes out. He is performing, putting on a disguise so that others see what he wants them to see.

Now, sometimes acting is just fine. We all love a good movie. Something with Denzel Washington in it. A good comedy. This summer's big blockbuster. In a movie, watching someone play a role is no problem at all.

But in real life, Care-Actors are a big problem. They do not have good character. They are imposters. The reality is, nothing a Care-Actor does is true, no matter how good it looks. He is a fake. An anime version of the man of character. He looks good on paper, but in real life, there is nothing of substance there.

An uncommon man is never content to be a Care-Actor. To be uncommon, you must strive to become a true man of character. To take off the disguise and be real...all the way to the core of who you are.

Developing Character

Of course, that is easier said than done. If good character were easy, everyone would have it.

But they don't. Maybe you don't. Maybe you want to have good character, but aren't sure how to get there. Maybe you have lost your integrity and want it back. Maybe you are, finally, ready to pursue true character, to become an uncommon man.

If that is where you are, I have good news. Character *can* be achieved. You *can* do more than simply play the part, knowing in your heart you are nothing like the person everyone thinks you are.

So how do you do this?

1. Build character, not a reputation.

Character is who you are. Reputation is what other people think you are. One is real. The other is perception. Character is built over a lifetime. Reputation is a snapshot, an action or decision that brands you, for good or bad.

Michael Jordan made his reputation as a clutch shooter when he made the game-winning shot against Georgetown in the National Championship Game during his freshman year. It was a single moment, but it was enough. With one perfect moment, he had a reputation that deemed him great.

Character, on the other hand, can't be contained in a single picture. You have to look at the entire album, taking into account lots of moments, lots of memories.

Michael Jordan's reputation may have been established with one shot, but his status as perhaps the greatest player of all time is based on his overall performance—in the regular season *and* in the playoffs, in practices *and* at high-stress moments. Over and over, time after time, MJ proved himself on the court. His actions confirmed his greatness.

And character is developed in exactly the same way.

You can do one thing with honesty and integrity, and people may think you have character. You will get that reputation. But character is a marathon, not a sprint. To actually gain true character, you have to work hard, every day, knowing that tomorrow you'll have to get up and do it all again. You can't get weary and let your efforts slide. You have to focus on the long-term, commit yourself for the long haul, and over time, you will develop true uncommon character.

2. *Focus on character, not talent.*

Talent is an innate ability, what you are good at just because you're you. Talent is a gift; you did nothing to earn it. And whether it's playing sports or teaching or acting or fixing cars, everyone has talent.

Think Tiger Woods. He has a natural ability to play golf better than almost anyone else in the world. If he is in the zone, he will blow the rest of the players out of the tournament seemingly without breaking a sweat.

That is talent. A natural ability to excel in a particular arena of life.

Character, though, is not like that. Character is not something you are born with. It is something you have to choose. It's something you have to work hard to develop. You may or may not be able to draw. You may or may not be good with kids. You may or may not have talent in a particular area. But you can have character if you choose to.

You can decide to work hard, make wise decisions and slowly develop the foundation of honesty, integrity and an incorruptible nature. You can't just give yourself the talent to play golf as effortlessly as Tiger Woods. But you can choose to develop good character, which will help you be better in every area of life.

In fact, if you choose to pursue character, it will add value to your talent, too.

Your talent won't get you anywhere if you don't develop it, and you will only develop it if you have the character to work hard and stay committed. In real life, talent may open the doors for your success, but character is what gets you inside. More importantly, character is what *keeps* you inside.

Consider Juwan Howard.

While most NBA players play for 6-12 seasons, Howard has been in the NBA for 20 years. As others dropped out of the sport, Howard continued to pursue his path with dedication and integrity. He has not been perfect. He has not always played well. But through hard work and discipline, he has developed a maturity and influence that is very rare.

This was clear in 2012, when Howard won his first NBA Championship with the Miami Heat. His presence on the team was more about character than talent. Yes, they wanted his experience on the court. But they needed his maturity off the court even more. Outside of basketball, Howard has served his community though basketball camps and Stay in School initiatives. He has worked hard, trained hard, learned from his mistakes. His teammates respect his character and experience, and that respect is what makes him a valuable member of the team, regardless of his on-court stats.[8]

Juwan Howard has talent. But his character has helped him develop that talent into a long-term, world-class career. And that is most definitely Uncommon.

3. Depend on your choices, not your circumstances.

Most people think circumstances determine character. Kids are assigned chores to "build character." Parents push kids into sports so they "learn good character." Unfortunately, that just isn't how it works.

Circumstances never create character. They can only display the character we already have.

Consider the basketball example I gave at the beginning of the chapter. The choice was to tell the truth and risk losing the game or to lie and probably win. Common character would say nothing. If the ref didn't see it, it didn't happen, and winning is more important than the truth. Uncommon character would tell the truth...no matter what it cost.

Whether you picked the uncommon choice is not the point, however. The point is that the circumstance itself would not determine your character; it would only display the character you already have. The guy with uncommon character would do the right thing, because he was *already* uncommon.

When I taught fifth grade, my students illustrated this principle every time I stepped into the hall. Some students stayed focused on their school work, studying as if I were still in the room. Others thought it was time to play because Mr. Brown was out of sight. With no one watching, some boys showed good character, and others showed they were only Care-Actors. The circumstances were the same, but the responses were clearly different.

The truth is...character is not determined by circumstances. It is determined by our choices. Look again at the proverb I shared earlier:

Watch your thoughts, they become words;
Watch your words, they become actions;
Watch your actions, they become habits;
Watch your habits, they become character;
Watch your character, for it becomes your destiny.[9]

Our choices about what we say and what we do become the habits that shape our character.

Each time you lie, it is easier to lie the next time. Every time you tell the truth, even though it costs you something, you make it easier to tell the truth again. Your choices develop and deepen your character. Making bad choices will result in bad character. Making good choices, repeatedly, will move you ever closer to the good character that will define you as an uncommon man.

The Importance of Character

The fact is...you cannot be Uncommon with Common character.

If you want to live uncommon, you have to make the good choices and do the hard work that will lead to true character. More than just crafting a reputation, you need to repeatedly live out actions and attitudes that are based on honesty, integrity and an incorruptible spirit.

Our uncommon identity helps us to move toward uncommon character. And our character displays itself in every area of our life, particularly in how we treat and respond to other people.

And that's why the next area we need to explore is...our relationships.

Discussion Questions

1. The short proverb claimed that habits become character. How would a habit turn into character?
2. What is the difference between having character and being a "care-actor"? Can you think of any examples of people who are care-actors?
3. Circumstances do not determine character; circumstances only reveal it. Do you agree or disagree? Why?
4. How important is it to have good character? Do you really need it to succeed?

Chapter 6

Uncommon Relationships

Let's Recap...Again

B eing Uncommon starts when you accept the challenge to value and protect your Name so you can pass on a true legacy to those who will come after you. Your uncommon identity will affect every part of who you are: your swagger, your friends, your character.

But your uncommon life will not simply stay inside you. It will begin to affect those around you, too.

Eventually, your decisions and actions and attitudes will be uncommon. You will respond in uncommon ways. You will begin to treat other people with uncommon courtesy. And nowhere is this change more important than with the ladies.

To be an uncommon man, you have to pursue *uncommon* ladies in *uncommon* ways.

The Hard Truth

BUT. Let's start with a basic reality of life: An uncommon woman is hard to find.

Oh, there are a lot of pretenders out there. Common ladies who wear a mask that looks good, but isn't who they really are. You have to look past all those common ladies. You have to search out the uncommon ones.

An uncommon woman has character. She's got class. She has uncommon identity, and it shows in how she treats herself, her body, and those around her. Most importantly, she's got uncommon expectations for any man who would like to date her.

And she does exist. You can find her. You can win her. But it won't be easy. Finding real love in our common world is very, very hard.

This is because you have to survive...the Love Game.

The Love Game is how the world does relationships and romance. It is based on common ideas and follows common rules. And it is nearly impossible to navigate it successfully. It is almost always a surefire method of ending up in the wrong place with the wrong lady doing the wrong things.

Here's how it works...

The Love Game

Common people treat love and relationships like they're some kind of TV reality show. Each player has to do crazy stunts, rack up points, and not get voted off before he finally "wins" the girl. It's a common mindset. It's a common plan. And it requires following these common "rules."

Rule #1–Get What You Can No Matter the Cost

These guys are all about themselves. They want something from their girl. They want the pleasure they feel they "deserve." They want "hot 'n' heavy," and they are willing to do anything or say anything to get it. These guys promise the world. They manipulate. They don't care who they hurt. They don't care how their girl feels or what it costs her. Getting what they want is the most important thing, and no cost is too high to pay for that pleasure.

Rule #2–Go As Far As You Can Without Any Cost

This rule is the "careful" rule. These guys are all about protecting themselves. They want to see how close they can get to the line (whatever that line is) without going over. They'll go as far as they can get without being caught or crushed. They'll go as far as possible while still avoiding any long-term consequences. Again, there's no regard for whether their actions cost their girl anything. They want to walk the line without crossing it. They want the pleasure with no cost.

Rule #3–Get Good Feelings Without Commitment

These guys are all about the physical. There is no concern for the moral or ethical or emotional side of romance. Getting in with their girl feels good in all the best ways, so they commit their bodies...but not their hearts. There's no commitment to the lady. There's only lust. There's no emotional connection. There's only sex. It's all about the moment, without any long-term view. They want to feel good for today with no promises for tomorrow.

That's how the Common man plays the Love Game.

It's all about him. It's all about feeling good. It's all about the moment. And it ignores the consequences. But...ignoring consequences doesn't make them go away. There are serious and long-term consequences to playing the Love Game by Common rules.

For more than a decade, I have been teaching in schools about dating, sex, love, and relationships. And I have seen and heard the consequences of playing by these rules. Countless girls have ended up with broken hearts; countless boys have been dropped to the mat by foolish pride.

When the Love Game gets played, someone always gets hurt. In the short-run, there is emotional damage to one or both "players." And in the long-term, both the guy and the girl are left disappointed and disillusioned. Having experienced nothing but meaningless relationships, neither one knows how to find something better, something fulfilling, something real.

Gentlemen, the common rules of romance are seriously wrong. They are hurtful. They are unkind. And they will never get you the girl of your dreams. Ever.

Leaving the Love Game

Thankfully, though, it can be different.

You can navigate the Love Game in uncommon ways. You can avoid the pitfalls and problems the Love Game will throw in your path. You can be part of relationships and romance that are real, serious, and beneficial to both the boy and the girl. It is possible, even in a Common world, to have healthy relationships that lead to uncommon love.

But before I tell you how that works, I need to be straight with you.

If you do love the uncommon way, there will be consequences. Some days, it will be very hard. Some days, it will just plain hurt.

To choose the uncommon path means opening yourself up to scorn, even ridicule. A young man who chooses to remain a virgin will be tormented by his peers. The other guys will tease him. They'll look down on him. They'll question his manhood.

And he won't get better treatment from the common ladies. A young man who refuses to hook up with an attractive girl faces another dilemma. If he declines for moral reasons, she may feel rejected and treat him with contempt. And when she tells the other guys, they'll accuse him of being weak, weird, or afraid.

Sound like fun? I doubt it.

But let me assure you. The rewards of uncommon romance far outweigh the cost. As bad as those situations may sound, as terrible as the teasing may be, pursuing uncommon relationships brings rewards that are beyond compare.

The issue is simple. The common way is shallow. Common relationships can never last. They have no foundation. They consist of two people taking from the other whatever they can get until both are empty, used up and disillusioned.

But an uncommon relationship is built to last.

Pursuing relationships by uncommon rules will result in strong bonds, connections that are based on respect and love. These relationships are real commitments, not short-term flings. They are more than feelings. They are strengthened by difficult times. Uncommon relationships are mutually beneficial: both the guy and the girl are better off for having been together. Even if the relationship doesn't last, the benefit of the connection will remain forever.

That is why it is worth the cost to pursue an uncommon relationship. You might be teased or tormented. But those few moments of pain will pale in comparison to all that you gain from the depth of the relationship created by the uncommon rules.

Choosing the Uncommon–Friends Without Benefits

So what are the uncommon rules for relationships? How do you get out of the Love Game and play for keeps?

First, begin by changing the **question**.

Common relationships are built on the question, "What can she give me? What can I get?" An uncommon man asks the opposite question. He challenges himself to provide instead of take. "What do I have to offer?" is the uncommon question.

And Gentlemen, you have much to offer.

You have the Name we talked about in Chapter 2. You can offer protection and provision. You can offer a woman a heart that serves, that gives instead of takes. And you can offer true love: more than feelings, it's a decision to always do what's best for your girl. That is how uncommon thinks.

Common relationships are built on the question, "How far is too far?" But in an uncommon relationship, the man asks, "How far can I stay away?" Not that you avoid her. Not that you refuse to get close. This question is not about withholding comfort or love or romance. This question is about value.

An uncommon man sees his girl as more valuable than a brand-new red Porsche. A car like that would be carefully maintained and treated well. That's how an uncommon man treats his lady. She is a treasure to cherish, far too valuable to use and toss like a paper plate. She is worth waiting for and nothing is worth trading her in for. That is how uncommon thinks.

Second, you have to change the **foundation** of your relationships.

Common relationships are based on selfishness and neglect. Uncommon relationships are founded on respect above all else.

Uncommon means that you always treat your girl with respect.[1]

In every way you can, you show her that she is important. You commit to learning *who she is*, not just how good she looks in a short skirt. You pursue her as a friend first, refusing to dive into the physical immediately. You aren't about using her; you value her. When you talk **to** her, you praise her. You ask what she thinks. When you speak **about** her, it is always with kindness and decency. She is never the butt of a joke or innuendo. That is respect.

And an uncommon man treats all women with respect. He refuses to stare at any girl's skirt because he doesn't want other guys to stare at his sister or his mom that way. He respects an older woman like a **mother**. He respects a woman his own age like a **sister**. And if she is younger, she needs to be protected like a **sister**.

So, you need to respect your girl. But just as important, you need to respect YOURSELF.

Guys, you are valuable, too. An uncommon man will not sell himself cheaply. No matter how good she looks in that top. No matter how hard she is throwing herself at you, YOU are worth the wait, too.

Sometimes we focus so much on the innocence of a girl that we ignore the immature thinking of boys. We encourage girls to stay away from the lustful boys, but almost no one is encouraging the young men to stay away from the promiscuous girls.

I'm telling you: stay away! Don't be a sucker. Don't be played a fool. Respect yourself enough to avoid being used. Be on your guard. Be incorruptible. Be prepared to avoid any influence that has the potential to damage or destroy you, especially when it is coming from a girl.

And how do you recognize a girl who's out to use you? That is the easy part.

A Common girl will ooze seduction. She'll be smooth and sweet. She'll look good, and she'll know it. But her words will be even more tempting than her looks.[2] She'll say all the right things. She'll talk about sex acts, and she'll talk about doing them *with you*. Her words will be flattering and make you feel good. But they are dangerous arrows, designed to bring you down to her level.[3] Most of all, beware her eyes. She'll be bold and coy.[4] She'll know when to glance at you and when to look you in eye. She'll use her eyes to call you over and encourage you along. She will have an arsenal of weapons to trap you, and she won't be afraid to use them.

Gentlemen, no guy on earth can withstand that kind of pressure for very long. Not one. That's why the uncommon path is so hard. To avoid that temptation, you may have to avoid the parties where those things occur. You may have to opt out of late-night hangouts and spend some weekends alone.

But respecting yourself enough to follow the Uncommon path will be worth it in the long run. A few weekends alone are a small price to pay for the freedom and reward of an uncommon relationship with an uncommon girl. Because once the damage is done, it can't be undone.

Don't wait until it's too late. Respect the ladies in your life, and respect yourself enough to follow the uncommon path. Pursue Love without the games. And enjoy the rewards of a relationship worth having.

Final Steps

The Uncommon life won't do you any good unless you let it affect your actual life.

When it comes to relationships, being uncommon means refusing to play the Love Game at all.[5] Practically speaking, to the uncommon guy, it is this simple:

Friends are friends.
Girlfriends are more than friends.
Sex waits for a wife.
Period.

There is no blending of the lines. There is no stealing from one group what belongs only to another. There are lots of friends. There is only one girlfriend at a time. There is only one wife for the rest of your life.[6]

That is how you play by uncommon rules.

The truth is, there should be no rush into romance right now. Yes, it feels good. I won't lie to you about that. But feeling good doesn't mean it actually IS good.

Having uncommon relationships means valuing the relationship, the connection you have with the other person, over anything else. Swear off the Common rules of dating and romance. Pursue a real relationship with an uncommon woman. Don't settle for something less.

You are Uncommon, and you are worth the wait.

Discussion Questions

1. What qualities or standards does an Uncommon girl have?
2. What are some practical things you can do to make sure you are not a Common guy, but an Uncommon guy in a relationship?
3. What does it mean to show respect to a girl in a relationship? Be specific and practical.
4. What are some ways that you can be sure to respect **yourself** in relationships?

Chapter 7

Uncommon Sense

Common is Good?

It's one thing to talk about being Uncommon. To talk about Uncommon identity or Uncommon swagger.

But talk is cheap. Talk is not enough. To be uncommon, you have to live it out. You have to walk the walk. Be the man. As Nike says...just do it.

So how? How do you live it out? What is the secret to living uncommon in the real world?

The answer will probably surprise you. More than anything else, you will need...common sense. That's it. There's no secret handshake. There's no special code. You need to develop plain old common sense.

But what is common sense? Common sense means making wise decisions, making good calls, using sound judgment. It's the ability to put into practice all the stuff we know we should be and do. It's wisdom PLUS basic good behavior.

On the other hand, I've been going on and on about how you should avoid common things. Shouldn't we avoid common sense, too?

Oddly enough, no.

In this case, *common* just means equally available to everybody. It's something every single person can have.

But having access to something doesn't always mean you make use of it. Lots of people have a piano in their house, but very few know how to play. It's the same with common sense. Even though everyone *can* have it, very few people actually do.

So common sense is uncommon after all.

The Value of Uncommon Sense

Common sense is rare, but it's worth having. Simply put, common sense is good for you.

First, common sense can protect you from bad situations. It can help you avoid physical, emotional, or financial harm. Someone with common sense knows that if something seems too good to be true, it probably is. So walk away. It's like the proverb says: "A prudent person sees trouble coming and ducks; a simpleton walks in blindly and is clobbered."[1] By walking wisely and listening to "that little voice in your head," you will avoid of a lot of trouble.

Common sense can also protect you from negative influences. Common sense says, if someone is bad for you, walk away. Takers, abusers, cheaters, users–someone with common sense knows to avoid their influence. At the very least, common sense sets clear boundaries. You may not be able to cut all contact with negative people, but you can limit their influence on you and your decisions.

Common sense protects our reward. What you put in is what you get out. Every time. No farmer plants corn expecting an apple tree to grow. It's never going to happen. The same is true in real life. What you sow (or plant) is what you will reap (or harvest). Common sense says to plant hard work and honest effort, so you can harvest your dreams. But if you sow laziness and lies, you will see your dreams fall apart before your eyes.

Lastly, common sense prepares us for real life. Common sense is practical. It's where the rubber meets the road. By developing common sense, we are prepared for anything that life throws at us. We won't be surprised by a sudden turn of events; we will have a safety net to fall back on, keeping our lives from falling completely apart. Common sense protects our real life.

Pursuing Uncommon Sense

So common sense protects us and prepares us for real life. It puts us on the path to success. But where does common sense come from? How do you get it?

By finding and applying wisdom.

Wisdom is "the ability...to think and act utilizing knowledge, experience, understanding, common sense, and insight."[2] In other words, you do what you know. We all need wisdom to succeed in life. We must have it to be uncommon. And thankfully, it isn't hard to find.

First, wisdom comes from the past.

To get wisdom, you need to read good books by good writers. You need to know how people used to think and live. Learn the lessons of the past, good and bad. You need to read proverbs and fables and stories with a moral at the end of them. You need to read. Read a lot.

You also need to learn your language well. You need to know what words mean and how to pronounce them. Develop a good vocabulary, not just so you can do well on the SAT, but also so you can understand what people are really trying to say to you. Slang has its place, but you must know how to use language well.

Talk to the older generations. These days, older men and women are not honored or celebrated. They are ignored and forgotten. But just because your grandfather won't use email or a cell phone, that doesn't mean he doesn't have valuable insights about life to pass along to you. Talk to older folks. Listen to their stories. Ask them questions. Let their wisdom become part of who you are.

I wanted my sons to understand this principle that no matter what their question or problem was, the older generations could help them through. I told my boys, "You may know the highways, but those men, they know every shortcut and back alley. They can get you there faster, and since they were around before the highways, they know the country roads that will get you where you want to go, even when the highway is shut down."

We can learn a lot from those who came before us.

Men like H. Leo Boles. A number of years ago, he gave a speech on the things successful men wished they had known before they turned 21. The list included some of the following:

I Wish I Had Known...That my health after thirty years of age depended largely upon what I ate before reaching the age of twenty-one.

I Wish I Had Known...How to take care of money.

I Wish I Had Known...That habits are hard to change after twenty-one years.

I Wish I Had Known...That things worthwhile require time, patience, and work.

I Wish I Had Known...That I can't get something for nothing.

I Wish I Had Known...That a thorough education brings the best of everything.

I Wish I Had Known...That honesty is the best policy for right.

I Wish I Had Known...The folly of not taking the advice of older people.[3]

This speech was actually delivered in 1928, but the list is as true today as it was 80+ years ago. Clearly the previous generations still have wisdom to share. Listen to them. Get their advice. Let them be part of your life so that they can help you succeed in an uncommon way.

Second, you need wisdom from today.

The world around you is a lot different than the one your grandparents knew. So you also need to find people who can help you navigate the right now. Talk to men who have walked the road just a little longer than you. They have wisdom, too. And you need to find it.

You need uncommon men to serve as your mentors and guides. Age does not always equal wisdom, so talk to people you respect in their 20s and 30s and 40s. Find out what they have to tell you, and take their words to heart.

Daniel Whyte III is one such leader. In 2010, he shared some lessons he had to learn the hard way, hoping to "save you many heartaches and troubles." Here's some of what he shared:

Things I wish someone would have told me when I was 12

I wish someone had taught me about the proverbial "value of a dollar." In other words, I wish someone had taught me how to manage money better, and how to save and invest it as well.

I wish that someone had taught me how to manage my time better. I wish I had learned the value of each minute of life at an earlier age. Time is like money – we must spend it wisely. Do whatever it takes to learn how to manage the time that God gives you.

I wish that someone had taught me to have a better work ethic. There is nothing wrong with hard work. Hard work is the road to lasting success. Learn to see work as a friend and not an enemy. Work hard and smart.

I wish that someone had told me, in a forcible manner, that junior high school and high school were not times in which to play, but to gain knowledge. I wish someone had told me that school and learning were a privilege and not something to be despised.

I wish someone had forcibly told me not to hang around the wrong crowd — that it was not cool — but rather, to be independent and to think for myself and to do that which was right. [4]

Anyone on the path ahead of you has wisdom to share. Ask what they've learned. Take their lessons to heart. They will help you live wisely and avoid the dangers and mistakes that they lived through and were affected by.

You need wisdom to succeed. And it is not hard to find. It is in the past. It is in the present. It is in the people around you. You have to look for it, listen to it, and put it into practice. Then you will become uncommon.

Getting Practical

Putting common sense into practice, however, is not always as easy as it sounds. "Just do what you know" isn't always obvious.

So now, we're going to get very, very practical. I'm going to get very specific about what common sense looks like in real life. None of this is hard. But it is very important. So here we go...

Common Sense and Personal Appearance

Choose to make a good first impression.

You only get to meet someone for the first time once. So you can't afford to mess it up. Once that first impression is made, it is very hard to change how people think of you.

Like it or not, a first impression is almost always based on our outward appearance. Our clothes, our hair, and our hygiene are the first things that people notice about us, and it will affect what they think. So remember: the way you present yourself, the way you dress, the way you cut your hair, they all say something about you, and you want that message to be a good one.

Of course, some guys want to blow this off. "People should focus on the inside, not the outside," they say. And they are right. What is on the inside is what matters most. An uncommon man will always make sure that his outside matches the inside.

BUT. People cannot see what you're like just by looking. They can only see the outside. And it's the outside that often determines whether they get to know you, whether they give you a second glance. Let's be honest. No one wants to talk very long to the guy who didn't shower after football practice.

You can go a long way towards making a good first impression by asking three questions before you leave the house.

1. Where am I going?
2. What is the appropriate attire for the occasion?
3. What do I want to communicate about myself?[5]

These questions, answered honestly, will help you create a basic look that will protect your first impression.

Of course, you can put your own spin on that look. You don't have to buy boring "grown-up" clothes. You can be stylish and trendy, but keeping these questions in mind will help you avoid extremes. They will keep you from ruining that good first impression with poor clothing choices.

But there is more to your outward appearance to consider.

What you look like is important, and you need to take pride in your appearance. Someone once said, "A man who doesn't care about how he looks doesn't care about much."[6] Even long after the first impression is past, your appearance can help you reach your goals, or it can keep you from them.

50 Cent is a great example of this. After building a solid reputation as a rapper, 50 Cent has moved into acting. But

his extensive tattoos were keeping him from the roles he wanted. So, he has chosen to remove some of his tattoos to help advance his movie career. He recognizes that what he looks like does affect his ability to get where he wants to go.[7]

The same will be true for you. Take your clothes, your style, your hair, your grooming and hygiene seriously. Appearances matter and they can make a difference in whether you ever achieve your goals.

Common Sense and Everyday Living

Common sense is about more than just how you look, however.

There are certain practical things you need to be able to do to succeed in the world. Many people cannot do them anymore. So it is worth your time and effort to learn these basics well. If you can do them...you have already become uncommon in these areas.

Handling Money

It's not enough to just want money. Having money is good, but if you never learn to handle it, you will never be able to use it wisely and provide for your family. Start right now practicing good money habits. Start with the Save-Give-Spend principle.

For every paycheck you ever get, divide your money into those categories. Save ten percent. Give ten percent of it away. Then spend the rest as you need to. You can always save or give more, but start now thinking of your money in those three categories so that, as an adult, you have good money habits in place.

Dressing for an interview

At some point, you are going to have to get a job. It will eventually happen. Whether it's mowing lawns or something much bigger, you need to know how to dress for that event.

Before the interview, shower and shave if you need to. Put on deodorant and maybe a light cologne. Remember that first impressions are important. So pick your clothes carefully. You don't have to wear a suit to a job interview at McDonalds, but you need to present yourself as a responsible and capable young man. Your clothes need to communicate that you are trustworthy and worth their time (to train) and money (to pay).

Common courtesies

Gentlemen, I cannot say enough about this one. Manners matter. Period. To be uncommon, you need to make good manners a priority. Manners communicate respect. Being courteous tells others that we notice them and we value them. A bad attitude or rude behavior says exactly the opposite. So hold open doors for others, especially women. Let others go first in line. Say please and thank you. Use proper table manners when you eat. Send thank you notes. Be a man who is known for his manners.

Because that is uncommon.

Conclusion

The uncommon life is a practical one. An uncommon identity and character will filter down into the everyday moments of your life.

Common sense is uncommon sense. And it is a valuable tool that will help you achieve success and dignity. Seeking out wisdom and applying it to your life will make others notice you, for all the right reasons. You will truly be Uncommon.

And it is at that point that you will finally begin to reap... the Uncommon reward.

Discussion Questions

1. Can you describe common sense? What is it? Why is it valuable?
2. What qualities should you look for in a mentor? How do you know someone will be a wise counselor?
3. Which of H. Leo Boles' "Things I Wish I Knew Before I Turned 21" do think is the most important? Why?
4. What other practical things can you do to make a good first impression in dress and appearance?

1. because if you dont have common sence you would be common.

2. Maker sure they are not a faker.

3.

4.

Chapter 8

Uncommon Reward

Defining Success

E very man wants to live a successful life.
Common and Uncommon, every single man wants to look back at his life and know that he succeeded. To know that what he did with his life mattered. To be honored for all that he achieved.

But what does success look like? How will you know if you've done well?

The common man thinks that success is determined by the amount of money, toys, women, power, or bling he has collected. In fact, most men are convinced that success means having more, doing more, being more, than everyone else around them.

But that is not success.

No matter what "they" may say, more money, more stuff, more women, more "fill-in-the-blank" will not make you a success. Success is only achieved by focusing on things that really matter.

Despite what common thinking says, heaping up money doesn't matter...creating real relationships does. Having more stuff doesn't matter...having true character does. Hoarding more power doesn't matter...passing on a true legacy does.

In other words, true success is only found in living uncommon.

Uncommon Rewards

Success comes when you do the hard work to build an uncommon identity, to protect your Name, and to leave behind a strong Nation. You have to choose to pursue these things. But when you do, you will harvest exactly the seeds you have planted. You will gain the ultimate reward.

You will achieve the uncommon life.

But...so what? Is it really worth all the work and sacrifice? What *is* the end result? What reward does the uncommon life bring?

There are three.

Uncommon Reward #1: Respect

An uncommon man will command the respect of everyone he meets.

Respect is a "sense of the worth or excellence of a person; the condition of being esteemed or honored; an attitude of deference, admiration or esteem; regard."[1]

To put it practically, when you respect someone, you admire him and treat him with honor. You listen when he speaks. You take to heart what he says. You imitate his actions, his words, his attitudes. You regard him highly.

And every man on Earth is trying to get respect. Every. single.man.

Like he needs air to breathe, a man needs respect to fuel him emotionally, mentally, spiritually. No man can be a real success if he does not gain respect, from himself and from others.

Unfortunately, most men are living without it. They feel disrespected by their families, their teachers, their bosses, their friends, even society as a whole. And they expend all their energy trying to get the respect they are missing.

But they are trying to get respect by common means. They think if they look just like everybody else, they'll be respected. If they get the hot girl, they'll be respected. If they make a lot of money, they will be respected. If they can appear powerful and rich, everyone around them will shower them with respect.

But it won't work. You cannot get respect by common means.

On the other hand, the uncommon life always leads to respect. People respect true swagger. A man with genuine character, who treats people with common courtesy, will be respected. The man who knows his uncommon identity and protects his Name always finds respect.

So what's the difference? Why does living uncommon earn respect? Because the uncommon man understands four ideas about respect.

1. Respect is **earned.**

Nobody *owes* you respect. You cannot demand it. You cannot force it. You cannot expect it. You will not be handed respect on a silver platter. Respect must be earned.

In my role as a father and husband, I could not just demand that my wife and kids respect me. I had to earn their respect. I had to make a commitment to being the kind of man they could count on, depend on, to be there for them. As I lived out that commitment, they came to believe it, and I slowly earned their respect.

The fact is, respect is always based on how you live. Talk is not enough. But when you think and behave in respectable ways, respect will follow. Of course, living a life worthy of respect is hard work. It takes discipline and dedication. But it is always worth it.

First, because you will be able to respect yourself. You will know the quality of man that you are, and you will be able to look the entire world in the eye.

Second, you will earn the respect of others. Those around you will treat you with respect. They will look at you with respect. They will listen to you, and you'll have opportunities to lead and serve.

Finally, you'll gain a reputation of respect. People you don't even know will treat you with respect simply because they've heard of the kind of man you are. That's what it means to earn respect. That is the reward of the Uncommon life.

2. Respect is earned **over time.**

Don't expect to get respect on the first day you commit to being Uncommon. It would be nice if that happened, but it won't. Respect is not an immediate thing. It is something you harvest. You have to plant the seeds of uncommon actions and attitudes and then let them grow, over time, until you reap a harvest of respect.

It happens in sports all the time. Some players come in full of promise and potential, but they falter, fall apart, in months or years. They seemed good at first, but over time, they showed themselves to be completely unworthy of respect. On the other hand, some athletes seem average, at best, when they begin their careers. But they dedicate themselves to their team and their sport. They play with heart. They lead by example. They have long-term staying power. And even if you don't cheer for that team, you can respect the athlete himself.

The same is true in every area of life. It takes time to build a reputation of respectability. Don't try to short-circuit the process. Keep sowing uncommon-ness, and you will receive your harvest in due time.

3. Respect is earned **by giving respect.**

Our actions determine whether or not we are respected. But our attitudes make a difference, too. Someone who achieves every success but acts like a jerk will not be respected. They may win awards and do amazing things, but they will not be high on anyone's list.

A real man earns respect by giving it.

When you treat everyone respectfully, you will earn lasting respect. This means treating others the way you want to be treated, regardless of who they are or what they can do for you. No mocking. No name-calling. No looking down your nose at people who are different or disabled. You see everyone as valuable, and you treat them accordingly.

Giving respect means that you are known for being courteous. You act like a gentleman. You make others feel welcome, special, and important.

And when you live this way, two interesting things happen.

First, you get what you give. The more you give respect to others, the more respect they give in return. Of course, we can't fake respect. The way we treat others must be sincere. But when it is, we will gain more respect in return.

And second, treating others with respect empowers them to be uncommon themselves. Mr. Burroughs, my fifth-grade teacher, treated us with respect. He held us to high standards. He challenged us. But he treated us as if we were valuable, and because he did, I began to see myself that way. The more I saw myself that way, the more uncommon I was inspired to be.

When we treat others with respect, we tell them that they have value, despite their flaws or imperfections, and our actions can inspire them to pursue the uncommon life along with us.

4. Respect is earned **by living respectfully.**

To earn respect, you need to live a respectful life. It has to characterize everything you do and say, particularly in regard to those in authority and those who have watch over you.

To be uncommon, you must respect authority figures: parents, teachers, coaches, the police and government officials. That doesn't mean you always agree with those "in charge." Sometimes they will fail; they will do the wrong thing. Sometimes you will have to work hard to change the way things work or the people who are in positions of authority. But living respectfully means you choose to respect their position as decision makers and rule enforcers, even though you dislike their behavior or attitude.

Living at this level of respect is a mark of full maturity. It is hard to respect a President you didn't vote for, but the uncommon man chooses to do so anyway. It is difficult to respect a boss or leader you believe is dishonest; it is hard to respect a teacher who is unfair and treats his students disrespectfully, but an uncommon man strives to behave with respect. Always.

And he is rewarded with the respect he needs to succeed. Always.

Reward #2: True Manhood

So the first reward of the uncommon life is respect. By living respectfully, you will earn the respect of every person you meet. But that is only the first reward.

The second reward of the uncommon life is to achieve True Manhood.[2]

A lot of guys think becoming a man is about some benchmark they have reached. They are a man because they're 18 or 21. Because they have chiseled abs or a million dollars in the bank. But that's not True Manhood.

For other guys, manliness just means not seeming "girly." They wear certain clothes. They do certain things. And it's all to make clear to everyone else that they are *men*.

But that is not True Manhood either.

Manhood is not about fame or physical perfection or accomplishments. Manhood is "striving for excellence and virtue in all areas of your life, fulfilling your potential as a man, and being the absolute best brother, friend, husband, father and citizen you can be."[3]

True Manhood is the reward of the uncommon life, and it always shows up in four specific ways.

1. A True Man rejects Passivity

Passive means sitting around, waiting for your mother to break down and clean your room. You could do it. You made the mess. But if you wait long enough, you know she'll do it. So you do nothing. That is not True Manhood. A real man is never passive. He does not sit by, letting others make his decisions for him. He chooses to act, for himself and others.

True Men are dominators; they are active. They participate in the spiritual and social responsibilities of their homes, their personal lives, and their communities. They are not abusive or controlling; instead, they are leaders. They set goals, make decisions (even the hard ones), and then do what is needed to bring those goals to life.

2. A True Man accepts Responsibility with Enthusiasm

Some guys do everything they can **not** to be responsible. They avoid every obligation. They want to be "free." But a True Man accepts responsibility: for himself, for his family and for his community. He does not avoid it. He works hard to meet his obligations and seeks to prove that he is capable of living up to the responsibilities he has been given.

But a True Man does more than accept his responsibilities. He accepts them enthusiastically. He doesn't slog through his days, moaning about how much he has to do and hating every minute of his life. No. He enjoys his life. He takes pride in his ability to meet his obligations. He wants his family and children to see him work hard, with a good attitude, to provide for those he is responsible for. He has his bad days, of course. But a True Man is positive and passionate, excited to live fully the life he has created for himself.

3. A True Man Leads Courageously

A Real Man leads, in his home and his community. He leads by example. He leads with a maturity marked by "tender-hearted strength, humble courage, risk-taking decisiveness and a readiness to sacrifice to protect and provide for the community."[4] He is a True leader.

But he doesn't just lead. He leads with courage. He faces bravely whatever comes. He has the courage to do what is right when no one is looking. The courage to work alone. The courage to live with truth rather than surrender to feelings. A True Man leads with courage, and because of that, people are always willing to follow him.

4. A True Man Expects the Great Reward

A True man, an uncommon man, keeps his eyes on the long-term prize. He is not distracted by the right-now temptations that sparkle for a moment and then disappear. He stays focused on the final prize, the great reward of a life well-lived.

And that life, full of meaning and community, is also Reward #3.

Reward #3: A Full Life

In Chapter 2, we laid down the challenge to live the uncommon life. To accept your Identity, protect your Name, and build your Nation.

And the final reward of the uncommon life is that you achieve all of those things. You develop that Identity. You add value to your Name. You have a true legacy to leave behind.

In other words, you find True Life. Real life. A full Life.

It's a life that any man can be proud of. It's not always spectacular. It rarely makes headlines. It is made of thousands of everyday normal moments. But when combined into a single Life, those moments give value and meaning to the person who lived them.

This life is not the shallow, fast-paced, shiny life of celebrity. It is not the show-off, expensive, self-absorbed life of the arrogant. It is much, much more. It is the well-rounded, deep, fulfilling and meaningful life of someone who lives wisely in the present moment to ensure a lasting legacy in the future.

It is the uncommon Life. And it is yours to live, yours to pursue, yours to achieve as you choose the uncommon path, the only path to true greatness, to true Manhood.

Conclusion

So we have now come full circle.

This book is all about changing your life, about becoming a young man who is ready to be the next great leader in his family, at his school, in his community and in the world. By following the principles in this book you will be empowered to live uncommon. You are now free to live out the Uncommon Life.

And that is our challenge. I am calling you out, pushing you to be better than the Common world around you. Dream bigger. Set higher goals. Go for it...act Uncommon, talk Uncommon, and live Uncommon, even in a Common World.

Discussion Questions

Chapter 8
1. How do you think a well-respected man acts?
2. How important is respect? How do you know if someone respects you? How do you know if they do not respect you?
3. How hard is it to accept responsibility with enthusiasm? Why?
4. What does it look like to lead with courage? Can you think of any examples of people who have been this kind of leader?

The Challenge: Becoming Uncommon
1. Do you think the rewards of being Uncommon are worth the work it requires to be Uncommon? Why or why not?
2. What practical things do you need to do to start becoming Uncommon? Are you willing to make this commitment and pursue this life? Why or why not?

End Notes

Chapter 1

[1]Matthew 7:24-27, English Standard Version.

[2]"32 Shocking Divorce Statistics." *McKinley Irvin*. 30 Oct. 2012. Web. 26 June 2013.

[3]Gretchen Livingston and Kim Parker. "A Tale of Two Fathers." *Pew Social Demographic Trends RSS*. 15 June 2011. Web. 26 June 2013.

[4]James Holder. "The Absence of Black Fathers in the Home." *Helium*. 02 Sept. 2009. Web. 26 June 2013.

[5]"The Consequences of Fatherlessness." *Fathers.com*. National Center for Fathering, 2007. Web. 26 June 2013.

[6]"George Washington Carver Quotes." BrainyQuote.com. 2013. Web. 27 June 2013.

Chapter 2

[1]"Most Expensive Hot Dog." *Guinness World Records*. 2013. Web. 28 June 2013.

[2]Proverbs 22:1, English Standard Version.

[3]"John Hancock." *The Biography Channel*. 2013. Web. 28 June 2013.

[4]"Nike Terminates Contract with Michael Vick." *USATODAY. com*. USAToday, 24 Aug. 2007. Web. 28 June 2013.

[5]Ryan Rosenblatt. "Nike 'Saddened' by Lance Armstrong's Doping Confession." *SBNation.com*. Vox Media, 18 Jan. 2013. Web. 28 June 2013.

[6]Chris Isidore. "Nike Suspends Contract with Pistorius." *CNNMoney*. Cable News Network, 21 Feb. 2013. Web. 28 June 2013.

[7]Shraga Simmons. "The Bar/BatMitzvah Guide." AISH. com. n.d. Web. 28 June 2013. http://image.aish.com/ BarBatMitzvahGuide3.pdf

[8]"Kennedy family." *Wikipedia, The Free Encyclopedia*. Wikipedia, The Free Encyclopedia, 22 Jun. 2013. Web. 28 Jun. 2013.

[9]"Archie Manning." *Wikipedia, The Free Encyclopedia*. Wikipedia, The Free Encyclopedia, 14 Jun. 2013. Web. 28 Jun. 2013.

Chapter 3

[1]John Calipari." *Best Quotes on Earth Blog*. 24 July 2011. Web. 28 June 2013.

[2]"The True Definition of Swagger." *Suit-Swagger.com*. 2009. Web. 28 June 2013.

[3]Steve Helling. "Kanye West's Bad Behavior: A Short History." *PEOPLE.com*. 14 Sept. 2009. Web. 28 June 2013.

[4]"The True Definition of Swagger." *Suit-Swagger.com*. 2009. Web. 28 June 2013.

[5]"The True Definition of Swagger." *Suit-Swagger.com*. 2009. Web. 28 June 2013.

[6]Fonzworth Bentley. *Advance Your Swagger*. New York: Villard, 2007: ix. Google Books. 28 June 2013.

[7]Blaine Bartel. Every *Teenager's Little Black Book on Sex and Dating*. Tulsa, OK: Harrison House, 2002. Google Books. 29 June 2013. 5.

[8]Fonzworth Bentley. *Advance Your Swagger*. New York: Villard, 2007: 3. Google Books. 28 June 2013.

[9]Matthew 7:12, English Standard Version.

[10]Tricia Ellis-Christensen. "What Is the "It Factor"?" *WiseGeek.com*. Conjecture. Web. 29 June 2013.

[11]"The "IT" Factor." *EON Sports.com*. Apr. 2013. Web. 29 June 2013.

Chapter 4

[1]"Friend." *Dictionary.com Unabridged*. Random House, Inc. 29 Jun. 2013.

[2]Proverbs 27:6, New Living Translation.

[3]Proverbs 27:17

[4]Thomas Wilson. *The Works of the Right Reverend Father in God, Thomas Wilson, D.D*. Oxford: JH Parker, 1860: 474. Google Books. 29 June 2013.

[5]"George Washington's Rules of Civility and Decent Behavior."*Foundations Magazine*. N.p., 2012. Web. 29 June 2013.

[6]1 Corinthians 15:33, English Standard Version.

[7]Proverbs 13:20

[8]Aesop. "The Bear and the Two Travelers." *Litscape.com*. N.d. Web. 29 June 2013.

[9]Proverbs 17:27-28, New Living Translation.

[10]Proverbs 18:24

[11]Proverbs 11:3

Chapter 5

[1]Kirk Mango. "High School Sports: Integrity In Sports–What Does It Really Mean?" *The Athlete's Sports Experience: Making A Difference*. ChicagoNow, 16 Nov. 2011. Web. 29 June 2013.

[2]"Character." *Dictionary.com Unabridged*. Random House, Inc. 29 Jun. 2013.

[3]Martin Zwilling. "Lack of Integrity Is An Easy Quality To Detect." *Business Insider.com*. N.p., 12 Jan. 2011. Web. 29 June 2013.

[4]"J.C. Watts quotes." *ThinkExist.com Quotations Online* 1 May 2013. Web. 29 Jun. 2013

[5]"Watch Your Thoughts, They Become Words; Watch Your Words, They Become Actions." *Quote Investigator*. N.p., 10 Jan. 2013. Web. 29 June 2013.

[6]Martin Zwilling. "Lack of Integrity Is An Easy Quality To Detect." *Business Insider.com*. N.p., 12 Jan. 2011. Web. 29 June 2013.

[7]Martin Zwilling. "Lack of Integrity Is An Easy Quality To Detect." *Business Insider.com*. N.p., 12 Jan. 2011. Web. 29 June 2013.

[8]Michael Cohen. "Leadership Helps Howard Contribute without Game Minutes." *Sun Sentinel*. N.p., 10 June 2012. Web. 29 June 2013.

[9]"Watch Your Thoughts, They Become Words; Watch Your Words, They Become Actions." *Quote Investigator*. N.p., 10 Jan. 2013. Web. 29 June 2013.

Chapter 6

[1]Job 31:1, English Standard Version.
[2]Proverbs 5:3
[3]Proverbs 7:21-23
[4]Proverbs 6:24-25
[5]Song of Songs 2:7
[6]Proverbs 5:15-20

Chapter 7

[1]Proverbs 22:3, The Message.

[2]"Wisdom." *Dictionary.com Unabridged*. Random House, Inc. 29 Jun. 2013.

[3]H. Leo Boles. "Things I Wish I Had Known Before I Became 21 Years Of Age." N.p., n.d. Web. 29 June 2013. <http://www.mabelvalechurchofchrist.org/gg/wishihadknown.html>.

[4]Daniel Whyte III. "Things I Wish Someone Had Told Me When I Was Twelve" *The Torch Leader*. N.p., 31 Dec. 2010. Web. 29 June 2013.

[5]Fonzworth Bentley. *Advance Your Swagger*. New York: Villard, 2007: 80. Google Books. 28 June 2013.

[6]Fonzworth Bentley. *Advance Your Swagger*. New York: Villard, 2007: 89. Google Books. 28 June 2013.

[7]"Why Is 50 Cent Removing His Tattoos?" *People.com*. 14 Apr. 2010. Web. 29 June 2013.

Chapter 8

[1]"Respect." *Dictionary.com Unabridged*. Random House, Inc. 29 Jun. 2013.

[2]Robert Lewis. *Raising a Modern Day Knight*. Carol Stream, IL: Tyndale House, 2007.

[3]Brett McKay and Kate McKay. "What Is Manliness?" *The Art of Manliness*. N.p., 16 May 2010. Web. 29 June 2013.

[4]John Piper. "Valuing Biblical Manhood." *Desiring God*. 23 Oct. 2007. Web. 29 June 2013.

Works Cited

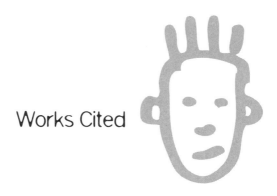

Aesop. "The Bear and the Two Travelers." *Litscape.com*. N.d. Web. 29 June 2013.

"Archie Manning." *Wikipedia, The Free Encyclopedia*. Wikipedia, The Free Encyclopedia, 14 Jun. 2013. Web. 28 Jun. 2013.

Bartel, Blaine. Every *Teenager's Little Black Book on Sex and Dating*. Tulsa, OK: Harrison House, 2002. Google Books. 29 June 2013.

Bentley, Fonzworth. *Advance Your Swagger*. New York: Villard, 2007. Google Books. 28 June 2013.

Boles, H. Leo. "Things I Wish I Had Known Before I Became 21 Years Of Age." N.p., n.d. Web. 29 June 2013. <http://www.mabelvalechurchofchrist.org/gg/wishihadknown.html>.

Cohen, Michael. "Leadership Helps Howard Contribute without Game Minutes." *Sun Sentinel*. N.p., 10 June 2012. Web. 29 June 2013.

"The Consequences of Fatherlessness." *Fathers.com*. National Center for Fathering, 2007. Web. 26 June 2013.

Ellis-Christensen, Tricia. "What Is the "It Factor"?" *WiseGeek.com*. Conjecture. Web. 29 June 2013.

"George Washington's Rules of Civility and Decent Behavior." *Foundations Magazine*. N.p., 2012. Web. 29 June 2013.

Helling, Steve. "Kanye West's Bad Behavior: A Short History." *PEOPLE.com*. 14 Sept. 2009. Web. 28 June 2013.

Holder, James. "The Absence of Black Fathers in the Home." *Helium*. 02 Sept. 2009. Web. 26 June 2013.

Isidore, Chris. "Nike Suspends Contract with Pistorius." *CNNMoney*. Cable News Network, 21 Feb. 2013. Web. 28 June 2013.

"The "IT" Factor." *EON Sports.com*. Apr. 2013. Web. 29 June 2013.

"Kennedy family." *Wikipedia, The Free Encyclopedia*. Wikipedia, The Free Encyclopedia, 22 Jun. 2013. Web. 28 Jun. 2013.

Lewis, Robert. *Raising a Modern Day Knight*. Carol Stream, IL: Tyndale House, 2007.

Livingston, Gretchen, and Kim Parker. "A Tale of Two Fathers." *Pew Social Demographic Trends RSS*. 15 June 2011. Web. 26 June 2013.

Mango, Kirk. "High School Sports: Integrity In Sports–What Does It Really Mean?" *The Athlete's Sports Experience: Making A Difference*. ChicagoNow, 16 Nov. 2011. Web. 29 June 2013.

McKay, Brett, and Kate McKay. "What Is Manliness?" *The Art of Manliness*. N.p., 16 May 2010. Web. 29 June 2013.

"Most Expensive Hot Dog." *Guinness World Records*. 2013. Web. 28 June 2013.

"Nike Terminates Contract with Michael Vick." *USATODAY. com*. USAToday, 24 Aug. 2007. Web. 28 June 2013.

Piper, John. "Valuing Biblical Manhood." *Desiring God*. 23 Oct. 2007. Web. 29 June 2013.

Rosenblatt, Ryan. "Nike 'Saddened' by Lance Armstrong's Doping Confession." *SBNation.com*. Vox Media, 18 Jan. 2013. Web. 28 June 2013.

Simmons, Shraga. "The Bar/BatMitzvah Guide." AISH. com. N.d. Web. 28 June 2013. http://image.aish.com/ BarBatMitzvahGuide3.pdf

"The True Definition of Swagger." *Suit-Swagger.com*. 2009. Web. 28 June 2013.

"Watch Your Thoughts, They Become Words; Watch Your Words, They Become Actions." *Quote Investigator*. N.p., 10 Jan. 2013. Web. 29 June 2013.

Wilson, Thomas. *The Works of the Right Reverend Father in God, Thomas Wilson, D.D*. Oxford: JH Parker, 1860. Google Books. 29 June 2013.

"Why Is 50 Cent Removing His Tattoos?" *People.com*. 14 Apr. 2010. Web. 29 June 2013.

Whyte, Daniel, III. "Things I Wish Someone Had Told Me When I Was Twelve" *The Torch Leader*. N.p., 31 Dec. 2010. Web. 29 June 2013.

Zwilling, Martin. "Lack of Integrity Is An Easy Quality To Detect." *Business Insider.com*. N.p., 12 Jan. 2011. Web. 29 June 2013.

"32 Shocking Divorce Statistics." *McKinley Irvin*. 30 Oct. 2012. Web. 26 June 2013.

Suggested Reading

Croyle, John. *The Two-Minute Drill to Manhood: A Proven Game Plan for Raising Sons*. Nashville: B&H Publishing, 2013.

Dobson, James. *Bringing Up Boys*. Wheaton, IL: Tyndale House, 2001.

Dungy, Tony. *Uncommon: Finding your Path to Significance*. Carol Stream, IL: Tyndale House, 2011.

Farrar, Steve. *How to Ruin your Life by 30: Nine Surprisingly Everyday Mistakes You Might Be Making Right Now*. Chicago: Moody, 2012.

—. *King Me: What Every Son Wants and Needs from his Father*. Chicago: Moody, 2005.

—. *Point Man: How a Man Can Lead his Family*. Rev. ed. Colorado Springs: Multnomah, 2003.

Johnson, Rick. *Better Dads, Stronger Sons: HOw Fathers Can Guide Boys to Become Men of Character*. Grand Rapids, MI: Revell, 2006.

Lewis, Robert. *Raising a Modern-Day Knight*. Carol Stream, IL: Tyndale House, 2007.

Rainey, Dennis. *Stepping Up: A Call to Courageous Manhood*. Little Rock, AK: Family Life, 2011.

Thompson, Michael, and Theresa Barker. *It's a Boy!: Your Son's Development from Birth to Age 18*. New York: Ballantine, 2008.

Weber, Stu. *Tender Warrior: Every Man's Purpose, Every Woman's Dream, Every Child's Hope*. Sisters, OR: Multnomah, 1999.

--. *4 Pillars of a Man's Heart: Bringing Strength into Balance*. Sisters, OR: Multnomah, 1997.